ACROSS **MANY** FIELDS
A SEASON OF OHIO HIGH SCHOOL FOOTBALL

BY CHRISTOPHER BUTLER & JENNIFER ROTHCHILD

Publishing Information

Library of Congress Control Number: 2002107277

ISBN: 0-936760-17-6

Published by Cleveland Landmarks Press, Inc.
13610 Shaker Boulevard, Suite 503
Cleveland, Ohio 44120-1592

Printed by Sheridan Books
Chelsea, Michigan

Cover and Interior Graphic Design: John Yasenosky

ACROSS MANY FIELDS

ACKNOWLEDGEMENTS

THIS BOOK IS FOR JOHN BUTLER, MY BROTHER AND FIRST FOOTBALL HERO.
AND FOR IRWIN ROTHCHILD, MY DAD, FOR SHOWING ME THE VALUE OF A PICTURE.

BECAUSE this book required us to impose ourselves on many high schools across the state, our primary thanks go to all the athletic directors who so willingly opened their doors to us. As if they didn't have enough to worry about on a game day, with all manner of grace, they also tolerated us moving in and out, asking countless questions, and pointing our cameras and microphone in every direction. As Ohio high school football is special, so are the athletic directors who make it happen:

Kirk Ballinger	Jim Hayes	Dan Moody	Reno Saccoccia
Bob Ballone	David Hoffman	Jim Offenbaker	David Sedmak
Dick Beerman	Dave Janofa	Barry Parsons	Donene Smith
Craig Boles	Dan Johnson	Norm Persin	Russell Smith
Lisa Bradley	Sally Kocher	Ron Price	Jerry Snodgrass
Kevin Calver	Craig Lefkowitz	Mack Rice Jr.	Myron Stallsmith
Dave Dabbelt	Michael Lillo	Jeff Riesen	Tony Triola
James Derrow	Ron Linger	Jim Riley	Bruce Young
Dennis Faber	Nick Magistrale	Matt Ritzert	Ron Zak
Phil Faires	Dan Merkt	Richard Roll	Doug Zimmer
Jim Gastin	Paul Mihalko	Aaron Roth	

OUR publishers, Gregory Deegan and James Toman of Cleveland Landmarks Press deserve more credit than we could possibly express. Their willingness to trust us provided opportunities we shall not be able to repay. With unflagging patience, they listened to our endless requests. Know that any shortcomings of this book lie entirely with us.

SPECIAL thanks also go to the Cleveland Foodbank, for its flexibility and support; to Kevin Butler, whose spirited support of our work and supreme editorial contributions surpassed all reasonable expectations of family duty; to Bob Goldring of the OHSAA for his repeated helpful assistance; to John Yasenosky for laying out the book with a superb professionalism; to John and Carole Butler, and Irwin and Ruth Rothchild — our parents — for everything and more; to Liz Deegan for her marketing wizardry and delicious cooking; to Frank "Digger" Dawson and Kevin Braig, for their enthusiastic support and friendship; to Paul Owczarzak, and Jim and Cathy McPhillips, for their company, photo reviews, and fax gathering; and to Katie and Sydney Deegan, for being so darn cute.

LASTLY, we would like to recognize the following people, who in some way extended a kindness to us during this long process. We hope that we may return the favors someday.

Dan Angelo	Dan Coughlin	Catherine Knop	Tom Redmon
John Ansell	Paul Cox	Jim Lanese	Tim Ridgely
Todd and Angie Baumgartner	Jon DeVore	Les Levine	Jon Rothchild
John and Jenny Birmingham	Jeff Dickson	Susan and Karl Lowe	Anne Sammelson
Ross Bishoff	Jay Dorhauer	Ben McDaniels	Corey Slavitt
Paul Boggs	Amy and Tom Elliot	Thom McDaniels	Ned Stechschulte
Sheila Brennan	Trent Evans	Mike McKittrick	Rick Thorp
Dan Brooks	Terry Fagan	Bob McNea	Shawn Valloric
Michael Burich	Jim Fedor	Tom Metters	Kevin Werden
Julie Butler	Jen Forshey	Tom Mullen	Thom Wojtkun
Gerri Butler	Robb Hemmelgarn	Larry Phillips	Brad Yoder
David and Allison Coho	Dustin Kadri	Charlotte Radler	

CHRISTOPHER BUTLER and JENNIFER ROTHCHILD

Since I was a young boy growing up in Centerville, Ohio football has been a central part of my life and my family's life. From my father's own career at Ohio State to my playing days, and current position with ESPN, I've been very fortunate to have football as a steady friend through the years. I've seen the ways it's forged bonds not only in my family, but within our communities.

I always knew that I'd be involved with football in my adult life. If I weren't working as a television analyst and radio show host, I'd be coaching somewhere, either in the college ranks or with an Ohio high school team. Simply put, football is where I feel most comfortable.

This connection is not something I take for granted. It came through years of hard work, dedication, and perseverance — three qualities football teaches very well. If I had to find the root of my commitment, or at least the moment when I first realized football's power on a personal level, I would have to go back to my own high school days when I played for the Centerville High School Elks. Two games, in particular, stand out in my memory.

In the fall of 1984, my freshman year, Centerville advanced to the playoffs and drew Cincinnati Archbishop Moeller in the first round, a tough draw. Ohio has many storied prep teams, and Moeller belongs in these ranks.

The Moeller High School Crusaders dominated the Ohio high school football landscape during the 1970s and '80s. Behind celebrated coach Gerry Faust, who would eventually go on to coach at Notre Dame, the Crusaders raised the level of play for the entire state. They wore flashy uniforms, dressed 120 players, and dominated teams who dared to step on the field. Many times, the Crusaders had the game won before kickoff.

I went to Galbreath Field in Cincinnati with five friends. We wore our black and gold Centerville jerseys, arriving at the stadium three hours early. We wanted to see every minute of the game, especially when Moeller took the field for warm-ups. We idolized some of their players like professionals — Tom Waddle, who later played for the Chicago Bears, and D'Juan Francisco, who starred at Notre Dame. The atmosphere was electric, and we were mesmerized.

The Centerville side of the field was packed by game time, despite a forecast of heavy rain. It seemed like the entire community was there. Early on, you could tell that our fans would be happy for any success. If the Elks forced Moeller to punt, we celebrated. If the Centerville offense gained three yards, we celebrated.

The skies opened during the first half, and the game slowed down. The game was score-less when Centerville's tailback, Dan Chillinsky, scored on a 27-yard touchdown run. We were stunned. It was like the moment when Buster Douglas knocked down Mike Tyson: the Moeller mystique was shattered.

Centerville hung on to win 10-7. Our fans cheered all the way back to town. The game fueled my desire to be a part of that atmosphere as a player. From that moment, I looked forward to when it would be my chance to play for the varsity Elks.

Two years later, we opened the season against Cincinnati Princeton, another southern Ohio powerhouse. At the time, if Moeller didn't win the state title, Princeton usually did. This year, their coach Pat Mancuso led a team of great athletes that featured at least eight Division 1 college prospects.

It would be my first start at quarterback. I would have preferred an easier opponent, but this was the moment I had wished for two years earlier. We fought hard, but late in the fourth quarter, Princeton scored to go up 21-14. We had two minutes to drive the length of the field. We did. Our fullback pounded into the end zone with just ten seconds to go. Our coach, Bob Gregg, called timeout. He could have ordered us to kick the extra point and force overtime, but he left the decision to us. Unanimously, we voted to go for two. I kept it on an option play. At the two-yard line, I was hit by a defender. I leapt into the air and stretched the ball across the goal line, earning us the victory. The postgame celebration was just like the Moeller game I had watched in 1984.

I do not share these stories for bragging rights or personal glory. I remember these stories because they were watershed moments in my life. I was able to carry the feelings of these games with me into my adult life. They changed me as a person and gave me confidence I can call on today. That's the unique power of high school football. It can transform young boys into men, and random groups of people into communities.

When you feel the collective hope of your town resting on your shoulders, when you find the courage and conviction to turn hope and hard work into celebration, you will know the greatness of Ohio high school football. I've toured the country watching foot-ball, and I can tell you that few places, if any, compare with the Buckeye State. As you read the stories contained in this book, I hope you will feel proud to be part of such an incredible tradition.

KIRK HERBSTREIT

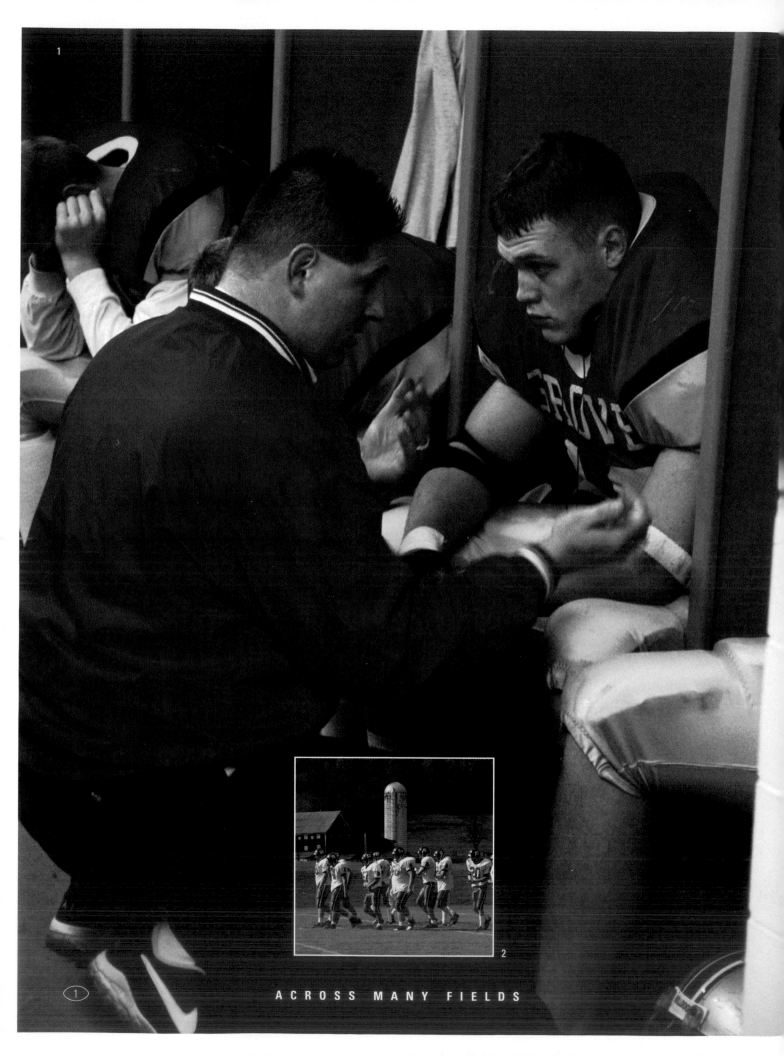

2

ACROSS MANY FIELDS

1. McComb v. Columbus Grove,
   Lima Stadium, 11/17/01

2. Newcomers Town at Bowerston
   Conotton Valley, 10/20/01

3. Locker Room, McComb, 11/17/01

4. Meditation at the Victory Bell,
   Marion Pleasant, 11/16/01

PREGAME

FIRST OF ALL, you're lost, and that's unfortunate because you've never been to this town before. You jumped off the highway, Interstate 71 (or was it 75? Or 70?), and barreled down several miles of rolling two-lane black top, fixing your stare on grain silos in the distance. Like working men, they peer out from the horizon, tall, ashen-faced, sooted by time and weather. Past the silos, houses begin to congregate by the side of the road, one at a time, swing sets and cars and front porches, and then bunches right next to each other, until you finally reach the outskirts of the town. The town introduces itself to you, and what's the first thing it wants you to know? *Division X, State Football Champions, 1981, 1985, 1992, 1998!* And below that, *Welcome to ——, population 10,003.* At least you have the right town. But now where to go?

That's your second problem. The Internet directions stop at the city limits. You continue straight ahead tentatively, looking left and right for signs and landmarks. The road leads to downtown, and you drive the strip, once, twice, a third time, and momentarily you wonder if you've wandered onto the set of an unmade sci-fi movie. The bank, the corner diner, the floral and gift shop, the library, the Twisty Top ice cream stand, and the playground — they're all empty. Only breezes and sunlight move with you down Main Street. You lower the radio and ratchet down the car's air conditioning. Swiveling your head back and forth, you notice the streamers and colored pennants and painted messages covering nearly every store front: *Beware! You've entered —— Country! Go ——! We're going to State and*

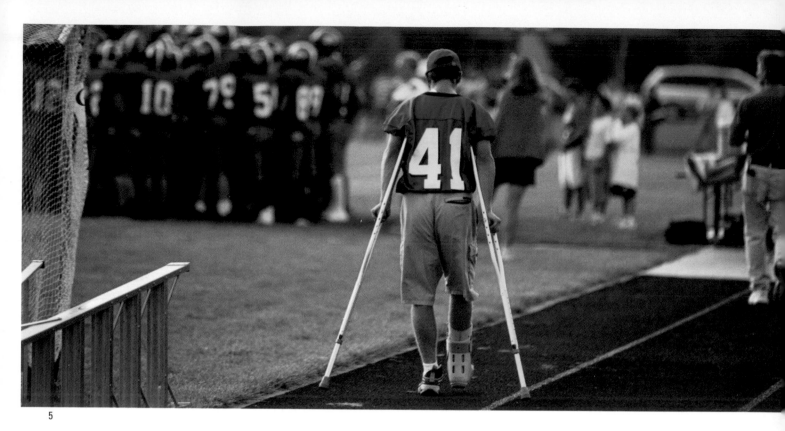

we won't be late! Come on Nelson, take us to the well, son! Direct warnings and strained poetry. More evidence you've found the right place.

You search for a school sign, the magic yellow diamond you hope will bring you at least

within hearing distance of the stadium. You know if you can find that diamond, you'll find people flowing in the right direction. One side street and another. No yellow diamond. You're losing hope, and you need to sit still and mull over your next move. *I just drove three hours to get here, and now I'm going to miss the game. I can't believe I can't find this place.*

You pull up to a curb and roll down the window, and there it is. It's a heartbeat, faint and distant, but regular and full like fat drops of rain … *boom … boom … boom … boom.* You feel it in your gut better than you hear it with your ears. Humid air rushes by your face, and now you smell it, grass and grain, sweat and perfume, popcorn

and grilled meat. The car jerks into drive, sets itself on auto-pilot and takes you down a street lined with maples and oaks that form a verdant canopy overhead. The drum beat grows louder, and the fragrance of cut grass wafts through the vents in your car. At the end of this lane, basking in orange light, the stadium opens up before you.

The parking lot attendant reaches into his cloth apron and pulls out a crinkly wad of bills. While you patiently wait, he wets a thumb with his tongue and starts counting the nightly take. Before you can ask for a spot, he waves you away with a quick shake of his

5. New Middletown Springfield at Poland Seminary, 8/24/01

6. Ticket Gate, Fred J. Brown Stadium, Defiance, 8/31/01

7. Harley-Riding Fan Club, McComb, 11/17/01

7

head as if to say, *You gotta be kidding me, pal. These spots disappeared hours ago. You gotta get here early if you want a good spot.* You manage to locate a space on the street about what seems a good half-mile from the stadium. It didn't look like the place could hold that many people, but you think you've seen enough cars for upwards of 40,000 people. This dampens your spirit a little as you think about what kind of seats will be left. Maybe you won't get the fifty, and maybe it'll be in the seventh row of standing-room-only behind the south end zone, but no matter. It's Friday night.

The throng pulses around you, completely unremarkable except for the way this crowd defies description or typecasting. Old people, young people, men and women, children and teens, all shapes and colors. They push toward the ticket gates with a purposeful walk. Children bound ahead of their parents, yelping and chasing after each other in a chaotic game of tag. Adults exchange hearty hellos and grasp hands eagerly, conveying excitement with every step. They wear t-shirts in school colors, carry seat cushions in school colors, and hold pom poms in school colors. Moms wear large photo buttons with their sons or daughters pictured in a stylized pose related to their evening roles — player, cheerleader, or band member. Dads wear baseball caps, some in shorts and others in jeans, and everyone dresses to be comfortable and cool tonight.

From inside the stadium you hear the band taking the field. The snare and bass drums rap out a steady cadence, setting the ranks into a march along the running track that surrounds the field. The band members stare ahead blankly, holding their instruments rigidly in front of them. Their steps are serious, precise, and confident. The drum majors march alongside with their fists clenched and held tightly against their sides, their

8

9

10

sequined epaulettes refracting the sunlight. Onward they advance to the end of the field, to their designated section in the stands where this disciplined group of musicians, in a matter of seconds, will dissolve into the group of young people they actually are. In the stands they giggle and yell and cheer and create an entirely different kind of music.

The traffic convenes at the ticket gates like cars before a turnpike tollbooth. People weave in and out of the crowd, jam on the brakes, and then speed up until there's no more room to wiggle; you're finally in line. Parents corral their children and pull out tickets or dig into their pockets for bills. Tonight's game will be five dollars. Just five dollars. And you didn't even have to pay for parking! The friendly woman in the booth, the one with the wizened face, who you somehow know must also work in the school's cafeteria, hands you a pass. This isn't one of those glossy bookmark-looking ducats with the team's helmet etched in bas-relief and your assigned section, row, and seat numbers marked in shiny ink. No, you hold just a red stub that reads (redundantly) "Ticket."

Ticket in hand, you try to orient yourself. Just where are you? It's all a bit confusing. You search the scoreboard for a clue, but it offers none. It looks like a plain old high school score board, ablaze with industrial light bulbs, and rimmed with colorful advertisements from various franchises. You look to the press box, hoping to see a banner or sign indicating whose field this is. Nothing — just weather-beaten white paint and tall windowpanes that look freshly polished.

You can stop your search right now. You'll not find any hints. Somewhere, somehow, you've slipped through the invisible fissure between time and space, leaving the tiresome

11

8. Town Support, McComb, 11/17/01

9. Store Front, Glouster, 11/3/01

10. Town Marker, Ironton, 11/2/01

11. Ashland Mapleton at Plymouth, 10/26/01

12. City Limits, McComb, 11/17/01

linear universe behind — at least for tonight. You've come to an extraordinary stadium, a unique field, a gridiron portal that will open up to you a flurry of football action, a veritable fountain of pigskin performance. On this supernatural night you are going to watch events from all the games of the 2001 high school season in Ohio, from week one to the state finals. These scenes will be culled from every corner of the state, from Montpelier to Marietta, and from Conneaut to Coal Grove. Tonight, everyone is here: 708 teams from all six divisions that play under the Ohio High School Athletic Association umbrella. In like fashion, fans, supporters, and staff from across the Buckeye State have descended upon this special place, combining their efforts to make this evening happen, to show why Ohio high school football is the best.

12

You glance at your watch and see that you've made it with plenty of time to spare. What was the worry for anyhow? You stop a moment and let the atmosphere swirl around you. The fading sunshine is warm on your face, and it seems to have a scent all its own. A raucous group of shirtless young men brush by, each one sporting a large painted block letter on his chest together spelling out the nickname of their favorite team. A group of young women follow in tow with glitter in their hair and wearing mesh practice jerseys from their brothers, boyfriends, and neighbors. Two young students cross your path, lugging a filled water cooler to the sidelines. Ice water sloshes over the sides with each step. The endeavor has become a desperate fight for balance amidst the whirlpool of people. Behind them a small girl with pigtails and sandals holds a Super Rope licorice with one

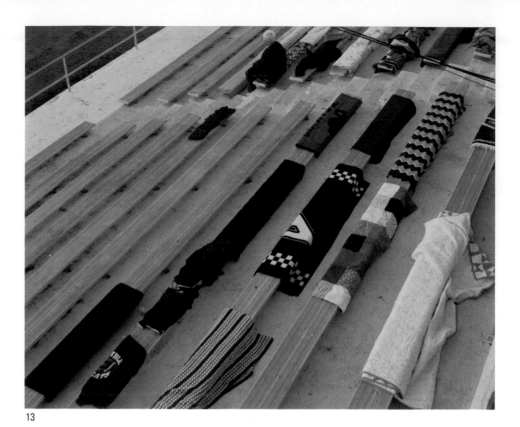

13. Reserve Seating, Trimble Field, 11/3/01

14. Reserve Seating, C.H. Jones Memorial
    Field Wellston, 9/7/01

13

end in her mouth and the other dragging on the pavement. This is the place. You've been coming to these games for years. Tonight you ask yourself: *Why? What is it that brings all these people together every weekend to watch high school football?*

"50-50! Get your tickets here! Split the pot and support your school! All the proceeds for the kids! Split the pot! 50-50, right here! Come on, Mrs. Randall. This game ball would look good on your mantle." Three men bark at the passers-by, trying to stir up commerce. Strands of tickets drape over their shoulders as they make change and small talk. Lynn Coleman of Fostoria sits at a card table behind them, hawking programs and booster club memberships. In Fostoria, young people attend Fostoria High School or St. Wendelin's, the local Catholic school. Coleman belongs to the Fostoria Athletic Booster Club, an organization that should not be confused with the Redmen Club, which sponsors Fostoria High School sports, or the Mohawk Club, which sponsors St. Wendelin athletics. The Fostoria Athletic Boosters sponsor both Fostoria and St. Wendelin, forming a noteworthy bridge over the church-state divide. Although you're not sure if this type of arrangement actually violates constitutional mandate, it is interesting to note that in Fostoria, athletics appears to supersede more mundane elements like law. As a past president of the Boosters, Coleman says he can't ever remember this being an issue.

Will and Clayton Holopeter brought football to Fostoria High School in 1895, but the team didn't notch a victory until 1897 because other schools in the area hadn't yet learned the game. Since then, the Redmen have racked up the third highest win total in the state of Ohio and sent a talented cadre of players into the collegiate and professional game. In a

good year, Coleman says the Fostoria Athletic Boosters raises between $45,000 and $50,000. Each year, the athletic directors for Fostoria and St. Wendelin approach with their requests, and the boosters make good faith efforts to meet every one. To raise the moneys they employ a wide range of sports-related events: Split the Pot, sports memorabilia auctions, reverse raffles at $100 a ticket (the winner of which takes home around $15,000), track meets, basketball and volleyball all-star games, program sales, and individual patronage. A quick glance through the Fostoria/St. Wendelin fall sports program — yes, they share that, too — reveals a list of approximately 400 Boosters and Super Boosters, a number perhaps even more impressive when you consider that Fostoria is a division three school, and St. Wendelin's a division six, the smallest school division in the state.

Just a few feet away you hear Armina Robinson tell her assistant, "I'm all out of programs. Can you hand me some more, please?" Her helper reaches into a cardboard box behind her chair and hands a stack of 20 to Robinson of Shaker Heights. The first time Robinson sold programs at a game, she netted $500, and the booster club president begged her to stay on after that. Because her son played for Shaker, she was more than willing to help out, but even after he graduated and her other son turned to basketball, she found herself still coming out to Russell H. Rupp Field on Saturday afternoons to cheer on the Red Raiders. That kind of devotion, Robinson says, was all about recognition. It was about recognizing what football had done for her son. As a divorced mother and a full-time nurse, she appreciated the values

"YOU GO THROUGH THESE STANDS TODAY, AND ASK HOW MANY PEOPLE HAVE CONNECTIONS TO KIDS ON THE FIELD, YOU WILL BE AMAZED AT THE NUMBER OF PEOPLE WHO HAVE NO CONNECTION WHATSOEVER. THEY'RE HERE BECAUSE THEY SUPPORT FOOTBALL."

Tom Rataiczak, Executive Secretary,
Ohio Valley Athletic Conference

15

16

the coaching staff instilled in her son. She watched her son develop a more serious attitude at home and school. In the off-season he landscaped side by side with one of the assistant coaches.

Robinson says she meets people from her own neighborhood at the football games, people who live only two and three doors away but who are virtual strangers. These are the same people who walk by her in the grocery store. At the game, they greet each other like old friends. In the stadium, the communal endeavor is understood — support your team, support your kids. Outside, it's a different story — we're too busy and have more pressing things to attend to. She calls it "funny."

Robinson makes your change, and you wade across the stream of people in front of you to the fence surrounding the field. Its lush green tableau makes your heart race. Imagine standing on that field and repressing the desire to break into a run. It can't be done. Plain impossible. It would be like standing at the edge of the Grand Canyon and feigning indifference. The last time you stepped onto an empty field, you were overwhelmed by an instant mini-drama: the snap, taking the pitch and running wide, looking for the friendly orange of the corner pylon, avoiding ghost defenders in a frantic dash for the end zone, the rumble of pursuers coming quickly from your right, footfalls that sound like approaching horses, the sidelines hemming you in, forcing you to turn upfield, straining for a higher gear, losing the angle with every step, leaping forward with the ball held in your outstretched hands, the rushing weight of bodies coming across your back, three, four, five bodies pushing you sideways in a rolling crash against the earth, tumbling outof-bounds, coming to a stop at the feet of fans and photographers gathered near the end

17

15. Ironton Tanks Memorial Stadium, 11/2/01

16. Granville at Baltimore Liberty Union, 9/28/01

17. PA Announcer Preparation, New Middletown Springfield at Poland Seminary, 8/24/01

18. Crooksville at Chesapeake, 11/2/01

19. Columbus World Harvest Academy v. Yellow Springs, Pickerington Stadium, 9/15/01

18

zone, their eyes wide and mouths open with muted excitement. Your head clears as you await a sign to render this calamity meaningful. The official is sprinting toward you, his arms raised overhead, signaling —

"Once upon a time, huh, buddy?" says a friendly voice in your ear. "Aw, hell, you'd a been dragged down in the backfield by the water boy," drawls another in your opposite ear. It's Steve Curtis of Lowellville and Lou Mains from Ironton. They clap strong hands on your back and welcome you to the field, taking particular joy in your reverie because they're the ones who laid down the chalk lines and hash marks. They understand and respect the dream-inducing allure of an open field, and they apply that care to their work. Like artists on a canvas, Curtis and Mains mark a field with self-assured and meticulous attention.

19

That afternoon, under a blistering high sun, they merged their respective talents and walked the field, pulling a contraption of wooden slats spaced a yard apart, and with long metal handles on each end. Slowly, steadily, Curtis and Mains moved down the sidelines, five yards at a time, setting the slats on the ground and spraying white paint in the spaces between. They passed the time talking about work and home and the game that evening, punctuating their banter with quick directives: *Down this way a hair … I'm good down here … Coach, another inch my way … I'm there if you're there*. And on they went, two-and-a-half hours, five yards at a time, sweat spreading across their backs like blossoming flowers. For tonight's game — in this special stadium — the field needs to look its best.

Having lived in Lowellville for sixteen years, Curtis still considers himself an outsider in his community of 1,300, which has only five roads leading in and out of town, three of those winding up and down steep, tortuous hills that you imagine become virtual bobsled runs during the winter. He picked up the field manager position at Paul Menichini Field after he was laid off from work. To occupy himself during the games, he started bringing a camera to snap pictures of his sons playing for the Rockets. One parent asked him if he wouldn't mind snapping a few shots of her son, and then another asked and another, and now he takes pictures all year long (his sons have graduated), assuming the unofficial role of team photographer.

Mains pulls triple-duty for Ironton as field worker, assistant coach, and teacher of learning-disabled students, although he tells you he'd gladly shovel dung if he thought it would help the team win. Working with one of the oldest and most successful high school programs in the state, he brims with unabashed pride when he explains that Ironton traveled 2,300 miles one season just to fill its schedule with games, so feared were they by local opponents. "We hit people down here. This isn't two-hand touch or flag. We play physical football down here." It's difficult to naysay his confidence. The Fighting Tigers have earned 20 trips to the playoffs, including 11 state semifinal appearances, six state runner-up trophies, and two state championships. This kind of success follows from avid support on and off the field. Mains, raised in the Catholic faith, underscores his dedication to the squad by attending

> " I LIKE THE TIME RIGHT BEFORE WE HEAD OUT AND WE'RE ALL DOWN AND HOLDING HANDS... WE BRING EVERYONE IN AND WE HOLD HANDS, AND SOMETIMES I TALK AND SOMETIMES I DON'T, SOMETIMES I JUST LET THEM GET A FEEL FOR THE MOMENT. WHEN I GRAB A PLAYER'S HAND AND YOU FEEL THAT PLAYER SQUEEZE YOUR HAND... IT GETS TO YOU...YOU KNOW?"
>
> John Keel, Head Coach,
> Teays Valley H.S.

21

22

20. Toledo Woodward at Toledo Libbey, 10/27/01

21. Delphos Jefferson v. Ada, Delphos Stadium Park, 9/22/01

22. Circleville at Ashville Teays Valley, 9/14/01

the local Baptist church over which the team minister presides. Mains says Ironton, an Ohio River town once borne up by the pig iron industry, has made football its "number one" business, netting approximately $75,000 a season after paying visiting teams $3,500 a piece for the trip. And that, says Mains, an Ironton graduate, is just from the ticket sales. The band boosters keep all concession stand receipts.

Curtis and Mains excuse themselves to attend to final preparations, although you can't imagine what they are. The field is pristine, the lines immaculate, and the crown at the center of the field looks perfectly set. Soon it will be the stage for tonight's performance, a soft platform on which drama, high comedy, and mystery will play out simultaneously. Through carefully orchestrated scenes with ornate costumes, the actors will fill the stage with music and movement. Though you've sat through hundreds of these plays, the anticipation still gnaws at you.

"Hamlet ends the same way every night. But with sports, you never know." You've heard that sentiment about football before, but when Terry Fagan says it, it sounds a little more true. He's propped against the fence a couple steps away, his blue eyes firmly set on the people that continue to push through the ticket gates. Fagan graduated from Cardinal Mooney in Youngstown, and you can't remember talking to anyone who knows more about Ohio high school football. What high school has placed the most players in the NFL? How many high school coaches in Ohio have led two different teams to state titles, and who are those coaches? What were the teams, and in what years did they win? How many high school conferences can boast of two state championship teams in the same season? Ask him anything. If he can't find the

23

answer in his head, he'll fish through the drawers in his filing cabinet, stuffed with newspaper articles and microfilm copies of high school football facts and figures. Or he'll turn to the Internet where in a few minutes he uncovers exactly what you want to know. In a thick Steel Valley accent, he dismisses your praise with force, but few

24

people can summon up statistics with his speed and accuracy. While his knowledge covers the Buckeye State, he'll always be partial to the Youngstown area. He tells you, "Frank Leahy, the old Notre Dame coach, once said he liked Youngstown kids because they're as tough as the steel they make."

You should start thinking about a seat. With your program tucked under one arm, you scan the bleachers on both sides of the field. It looks as if you'll be lucky to get a spot beneath the stands at this point, squatting among the emptied cups, popcorn boxes, and candy wrappers that unintentionally (and intentionally) fall through the seats. From goal line to goal line, people have packed themselves in tightly, using every available inch of space like riders on a Tokyo subway train. Skinny people share one seat, parents hold small children in their laps, people turn sideways into the aisles, careful not to grab the attention of local police officers on whom falls the unenviable task of keeping the aisles clear.

There is, however, something unsettling about tonight's crowd and how it lies before you. It's the color. The color of the clothing. No one color dominates this crowd. Instead, it's a pixilated mish-mash of hues. Here and there you find pockets of red, or

25

23. Lincoln West v. Cleveland East, Patrick Henry Field, 11/12/01

24. Lorain Southview at Shaker Heights, 10/13/01

25. Gnadenhutten Indian Valley at Uhrichsville Claymont, 10/27/01

pockets of blue or green or gold. But only pockets. For contrast, consider a home game at Elder High School in Cincinnati where visitors to the legendary "Pit" find themselves feeling clothed but strangely naked if they aren't wearing something purple. Purple sweaters, purple caps, purple shirts, even purple wigs. One popular t-shirt reads, "It's a purple thing. You wouldn't understand." Well, you sort of understand. School colors. They serve as your sign, like coats-of-arms in the British Isles. At Elder it's purple: the venerated color on the corner of Regina and Vincent avenues, perhaps inspired by the royal purples of Catholic priestly garb. Purple: the Elder Panthers and their supporters live here.

Tonight, you have a mission, a personal one. You want to learn why Ohio high school football is, beyond dispute, tops in the country. You want to get at the scratch beneath the contest, to uncover the patterns and motivations that bring us out, faithfully, every weekend, to scream ourselves hoarse, to endure bone-chilling rains and frozen aluminum benches, to donate our time, effort, and money, to freely give our emotions over to the performances of 16- and 17-year-old kids, and to promise to do it all over again next week and next year and the year after that. Yes, you've heard arguments on behalf of other states — Pennsylvania, Texas, Florida, California — but you know there's no state where high school football forms a more vibrant part of its culture. Maybe this sounds crazy to you, and maybe it doesn't, but one thing is for sure: It's an Ohio thing; people in the Buckeye state understand; and everyone's welcome.

Certainly John Przelenski would understand your mission. He lives in Charlotte, North Carolina, and officiates high school football games in Ohio. That's right. Six, seven

26

26. New Middletown Springfield at
    Poland Seminary, 8/24/01

27. Lakewood St. Edward v. Cleveland
    St. Ignatius, Lakewood Stadium, 10/13/01

28. Circleville at Ashville Teays Valley, 9/14/01

29. Obie 32, Massillon Washington Mascot,
    Paul Brown Tiger Stadium, 11/23/01

times a season, Przelenski makes the eight-hour haul up Interstate 77 just so he can don the stripes and polyester white pants and step onto the field of an Ohio high school football game. Yes, they play football in North Carolina, but it doesn't suit his tastes. North Carolina football, he says, relies on finesse and trickery, a style that differs too much from

27

the hard-nosed game he knew growing up in the Ohio Valley region. Of course, this is not to say that Przelenski, an official now for more than 20 years, enjoys the long commute and vast array of fast food stops between here and Charlotte. He patiently stands by in his current job waiting for a transfer. But until then, he looks ahead to each late summer when he can start planning those long journeys just to be in the midst of a high school football game on a Friday night in Ohio.

It doesn't appear that you're going to have anywhere to sit, but you might as well take a look. Walking along the fence in front of the stands, you spy various team assistants busying themselves around a couple wooden tables set up behind the sideline benches. On one table, young men and women in t-shirts and beige shorts fill green paper cups and blue squirt bottles with water. One young woman sits on the ground kneading the kinks in a tangled mess of thin cable as her "helper" stands nearby holding two headsets and waving to her parents in the stands.

At the other table, team trainers spread out their wares, making sure they have all the necessary supplies for the evening: tape, ACE bandages, gauze, scissors, smelling salts, adhesive bandages, topical disinfectant, and sterilized latex gloves. Minutes ago, in the

bowels of the locker room, underneath the oppressive blare of heavy metal warbling hellishly through the speakers of a paint-spattered boom box, on examining tables with cracked naugahyde coverings, the trainers finished their pregame ritual, taping ankles, taping knees, applying medicated balm to stiff joints and sore muscles, giving players final instructions about how to treat their ailments in case they flare up during the contest. They hand out these directions earnestly, but most of the players don't hear much at this point, already immersed in their pregame hype. They're young, these trainers, typically ex-athletes themselves, mostly fresh from college, putting in grunt years before they move on to universities and hospitals where the pay increases substantially. They work 20 hours a week with the schools and attend all the games in addition to holding down extra employment just to make ends meet.

A little farther down the fence you encounter a pack of cheerleaders fastening strips of crepe paper to the front railings of the stands. Just like the team they'll soon be cheering for, they strike a uniformity of appearance: pony tails, glitter makeup, glitter in the hair, matching bows and ribbons, ankle-cut socks, and white aerobic shoes. Their canvas duffel bags are piled along the fence, spilling over with items of anticipation and preparation — sweatshirts, rain pants, cosmetic kits, good luck charms, packs of chewing gum, extra ribbons, and Walkmans. During the pregame, they scatter about the track in smaller groups, stretching, socializing, reviewing the evening's routines, and wondering about postgame parties and weekend homework assignments. Watching them work and chat now at such

a dizzying pace — a truly impressive display of human electricity — you wonder why the government hasn't considered a way of tapping their energy as a national resource. On the surface, it may seem more levity than leverage for these young women, but don't underestimate their devotion to the cause. This group arrived at 2 p.m. for a 7:30 game and set about decorating the stadium with hand-made posters, helium-filled balloons and, of course, streamers in team colors.

"YOU KNOW WHAT WATER IS? YOU KNOW WHAT BLOOD IS? WELL, BLOOD'S THICKER THAN WATER. THAT'S WHY I'M OUT HERE, RAIN OR SHINE."

Merrill Hunt, Grandfather of Player, Cheaspeake H.S.

Lindsay Wiley and Holly Cowles work in concert, moving steadily down the row, one with the tape, the other with a roll of crepe paper. They cheer for the Spartans of Marion Pleasant and take great pride in their place within the football universe of the school. It's all a system, they tell you. If the team is down, then the crowd is down. It falls, then, to the cheerleaders to get the crowd going, and when the crowd gets going, the team plays better, and when the team plays better, the crowd becomes more excited, and when the crowd is more excited, then the cheerleaders have more fun. Perfect, unbreakable circularity here at the stadium. Their duties, however, are not confined to the weekend. During the week, the Spartan cheerleaders practice and choreograph new routines, run through conditioning drills, decorate players' lockers, and organize pep rallies for the important games of the year. Some cheer-leaders will reluctantly admit that many people are not aware of the level of commitment required for their sport, but they keep that grievance to themselves, determined to keep spirits high in the stadium.

32

A low rumble billows from the corner of the stadium and spreads over the crowd like an invisible tidal wave. A team has been spotted, preparing to take the field for calisthenics and pregame drills. The young men file out of the locker room two-by-two, like creatures boarding Noah's Ark. The cleats on concrete sound like tap shoes as they stare ahead rigidly, affecting focus and mental toughness. The leaders stop at the gate and wait for the entire team to assemble behind them. With quiet power, they proceed onto the field, keeping the orderly ranks. Ten by ten, with quick breaks, the team divides into rows, lining up every five yards. A few players put an extra hop into their turn, barely containing their desire to play and whoop and get past this stifling ritual of stretch, drill, and walk through. Others step diffidently and round off the corners, usually the younger players who are still adjusting to this elevated level of psychological intensity, still trying to find a rhythm within this regimented show of enthusiasm.

33

Team captains bark and their teammates respond. They stand and stretch, sit and stretch, partner up and stretch some more, pulling arms and legs forward and back and every which way. Coaches wander in and out, leaving stray remarks every few feet. *It's time to get your head in the game! What have you been working for all year? The time is now, gentlemen. The time is now! Are you gonna let these guys push you around? On your own field? We're gonna take it to 'em right away! From the first play, we're gonna let them know we can hit! Right, Nelson? You hear me, Nelson?* Nelson: *Yes, sir.*

34

34. Wellston v. Waverly, C.H. Jones
    Memorial Field, 9/7/01

35. Kenton v. Coldwater, Findlay Donnell
    Stadium,11/24/01

36. Cincinnati St. Xavier v. Cincinnati
    Princeton, Paul Brown Stadium, 11/10/01

37. New Philadelphia Tuscarawas
    Central Catholic v. Malvern,
    Dover, Crater Stadium, 9/29/01

Gradually, the players shed the steely exterior, popping off the ground with extra zeal, showing a little more of the boy inside, preparing for that moment when they can finally burn off the nervous energy that has been roiling inside since Thursday morning.

35

As calisthenics conclude, the team momentarily resembles a disrupted ant farm with players running every which way to different corners of the field. Backs, linemen, backers, ends, skill players, and special teams spread within the team's 50-yard allotment. J.E. Kirkpatrick, a volunteer assistant coach for Reedsville Eastern High School, gathers his offensive linemen and directs them through short agility and contact drills. He moves and speaks with the enthusiasm of the players under his command. *On the ball, on the ball! Fire out fire out! Be the hitter, not the hittee! Set! Go! Set! Go! Reverse it! Set! Go!* A former lineman himself who played for the Seattle Seahawks, Kirkpatrick says high school football is 20 percent ability and 80 percent emotion, and watching him rally his players, you see that he tries to pull that emotion out. Since his high school playing days nearly 20 years ago, he is struck by the off-season dedication young men now have to football. At Eastern, he says the players have adopted year-round weightlifting and conditioning, and the extra work is paying dividends for the team. The 2001 season marked Eastern's second straight trip to the state playoffs, and just the second trip in school history. Kirkpatrick says the off-season work has raised the overall athleticism of the team, making his job a bit easier: "You can teach kids how to block, but you can't make

36

37

them faster. You can teach them whom to block, but you can't always send out a kid who benches 300 pounds."

In an opposite corner, Scott Boggs watches intently as the quarterbacks from Delphos Jefferson take practice snaps from center, getting a feel for the ball. A Jefferson alum and former quarterback himself, Boggs started coaching at the request of his head coach, Jim Morris, and has been with the team now for seven years. Delphos is a northwestern town of approximately 8,000 people, well known for fielding two excellent high school teams despite a relatively small population. The Catholic school, St. John's, has won several state titles while establishing itself as a perennial contender for over a decade. Jefferson also enjoys regular success and, with Boggs at quarterback, made a trip to the state finals in 1986 where it lost to state power Newark Catholic. When the Wildcats arrived back in Delphos, feeling dejected and responsible, he says the town folk lined Main Street and threw a big celebration for the team. "They were more excited than we were," he remembers.

Boggs credits the town's football success to the strong youth leagues organized largely by parents and interested adults. The players he coaches now seem to know much more about the game than when he was their age. Another reason for the success is the proliferation of coaches at all levels. When Boggs played junior high, he says the team had one head coach and one assistant to direct the team. Today's junior high team at Jefferson has five coaches and a small crew of dads helping out in their spare time.

While Delphos supports two successful teams in peaceful co-existence, St. John's and Jefferson had resisted playing each other for over 30 years. Most people tell you it's because the teams play in different divisions and conferences (St. John is Division 6 and the Midwest Athletic Conference, Jefferson in Division 5 and the Northwest Conference), but you suspect that's a convenient excuse to spin when it comes to preserving healthy relations between the families that have been sending generations of children through each school. Last year, however, St. John's male enrollment grew enough to warrant moving up one division, a development that caused town leaders and administrators to worry, while team supporters on both sides rubbed their hands together in unrestrained excitement, hoping for the oft-speculated but never realized Civil War of Delphos. It must have seemed like football destiny when both teams put together successful seasons and found themselves paired against each other in the first round of the playoffs. Even though state rules would allow the higher seed (in this case, Jefferson) to host this game, Delphos Stadium Park, it was said, could not hold the anticipated crowds for this match-up, so the game was moved to a larger stadium southeast of town. During the week preceding the game, people joked to each other about assigning someone to turn off the lights on Friday night when the entire town would caravan down state route 309 to Lima. All the what-ifs and yeah-buts were laid to rest that evening, at least for one year, when St. John's prevailed in the inaugural contest, 38-13.

After 15 minutes of drills, the position players gather around their coach, hopping and stamping their feet like penned-in horses. Little by little, the energy levels have risen, simmering now, barely containable. They all raise one arm and clasp hands overhead. The coach, ensconced in this protective circle of youthful drive and passion, snaps out

38. Cincinnati St. Xavier v. Cincinnati Princeton, Paul Brown Stadium, 11/10/01

39. Avon Lake at Amherst Steele, 10/12/01

39

40. Steubenville v. East Liverpool, Harding Stadium, 10/19/01

41. Granville at Baltimore Liberty Union, 9/28/01

40

final encouragement to his players. *The linebackers lead the defense. Remember what we talked about this week in practice. You guys set the tone. Make that first big hit! Set the tone! Let them know they're in for a long night! Show your teammates you're here to play! You hear me? Make that first hit! All right, all right, on the break. Hands together. 1-2-3. Break!*

Sounding their barbaric yawp, the players come together in the end zone to run through some final offensive and defensive sets. Coaches mill nervously about on both sides of the ball looking for any final adjustments that need to be made, any fine point that might help their players: a shortened step, a sharpened angle, any small movement that might give their team another inch, another yard, another score. They know this proverbial "game of inches" starts as a game of position and technique. Poor technique + bad position = fewer inches, fewer yards, fewer scores. Watching them move around in a trance-like state, you think some of them might chew holes in their faces if it weren't for the invention of bubble

41

gum. The players line up on both sides of the ball, their bodies looser, even a little slack, as they grow a tad more impatient for the real thing. The quarterback hands off to a waiting running back as the linemen square against each other, arms extended, facemask to facemask, just making contact for a few seconds until the back scurries past into the defensive backfield where he's butted up by players waiting there, eager for contact.

The teams run through plays methodically for ten minutes before the head coach signals for a retreat into the locker room. The band springs to life with a rousing fight song. The

42

42. Avon Lake at Amherst Steele, 10/12/01

43. Dayton Meadowdale v. Portsmouth,
    Dayton Welcome Stadium,10/6/01

44. Piqua at Troy, 9/21/01

45. Reedsville Eastern at Glouster Trimble,
    11/3/01

crowd rises to its feet watching the players jog off the field, knowing that when they return, the show will begin. When the players return, the curtain will be up. When the players return, their uniforms will be clean and fresh, shirts tucked in, helmets polished and glistening underneath the high spotlights. When the players return, all emotions

43

will be powerful and expectant. When the players return, the stands will transform from cocktail party to cheering section. When the players return, everyone, from the on-duty paramedics to the assistant band director, will meld individual interests into a consuming collective resolve for victory, fun, and an injury-free game.

From the far end zone you spot another group of cheerleaders approaching arm in arm. They've come from the other side of the field where they've completed their preparations and have now decided to engage in the traditional pregame greeting of the opposing cheerleaders and fans. The young women mix and natter and compliment each other profusely, teeming with nervous energy, their ponytails rapidly bobbing up and down. After a minute of pleasantries the home group backs away, allowing the visitors to execute their opening cheer, an energetic chant of introduction and good will. The team lines up in two rows, eight young women across. They hold themselves perfectly still, chins tucked down, hands clasped tightly into their chests, feet shoulder width apart. *Ready … We! Would like! To welcome you!* Step forward. *Welcome you!* Step forward. *Welcome you!* Step forward, spin. *We! Would like! To welcome you!* Step forward. *Welcome you!* Step forward. *Welcome you!* Step forward, spin. Clap-clap-clap-clap.

The crowd responds with hearty applause, and the home cheerleaders bound forward to congratulate their colleagues. A second short round of compliments and compliment deflection ensues, and the young women link arms again and head around the track to the opposite bleachers, where they will enact this scene in reverse fashion, another sign that the game is nigh.

Minutes earlier, as final drills took place, team captains were brought to midfield for the coin toss, the lone moment of the evening intentionally left to the whims of plain luck. After this flip of the quarter, human factors will preside over the course of play. Four captains a side, facing each other, they pull off their helmets and await instructions. The referee assumes the role of temporary party host, asking the players to introduce themselves to each other. Some boys use affable grins with loose handshakes while others remain stone faced and mechanical. Regardless of style, all of them wear transparent faces, barely concealing the nervousness, the chunks of ice swelling deep inside their stomachs, that feeling inaccurately known as "butterflies." Eyebrows twitch, sweat runs down cheeks and foreheads, and nostrils flare unconsciously. They mumble greetings to each other and quickly fall back into line.

The other officials stand opposite the referee in a tidy row, four across. Although they all have perfectly good names, they will be known tonight as back judge, line judge, linesman, umpire, and referee. The crew chief — the referee — breaks into a traditional preamble:

46

46. Piqua at Troy, 9/21/01

47. Ashtabula Edgewood at
    Hanoverton United, 8/25/01

48. Struthers at Niles McKinley,
    10/11/01

"Gentlemen, we are your best friends tonight. We're going to help you if you help us. We're going to keep this game clean, and we're not going to talk back to the officials or each other. If you have something to say, say it to your coach, and he'll tell us. Those are the lines of communication tonight. All right?

"Starting from the left, that's Mr. John Evans..." One by one, the officials step forward and doff their caps.

> "... Good luck tonight, guys."
>
> "Next to him is Mark Peterson ..."
>
> "... Let's have fun tonight, guys."
>
> "The side judge will be Ken Kazerman ..."
>
> "... Good luck tonight, gentlemen."

When the introductions are finished, the referee asks the visiting team captain to call the toss. He instructs the young man to call heads or tails while the coin is in the air. He carefully displays both sides of the coin and tosses it neatly in the air, all eyes fixed intently on the short parabola of the coin's flight. On its way down the referee claps it together between his palms and issues the first edict of the night: "It is tails. The home team has won the toss. They will choose to kick off or receive."

After the choice is made, the referee moves the captains one way or the other to show who will kick off and which team will play to which side. It's a courtesy for the spectators and a point of strategic departure for the coaches. From this point, the coaching staff has its first clue, the first morsel of information to begin settling the week's endless

47

48

conjecture: *What if they come out in a fifty front? What if they overload one side of the line? What if they go to a full house backfield? What if they drop two safeties on first down?* The coaches know exactly one thing now: who has the ball first.

Inside the locker room, the team waits anxiously for the start of the game. A few players strut back and forth, fuming intensity. Others sit on benches, legs jittering up and down, cleats sounding rapid-fire on the cement floor. Team captains issue final statements, less of instructional worth than inspired repetition.

D.J. Ogilvie steps to the front of the room to address his team from Hanoverton United. The youthful-looking head coach of the Golden Eagles starts quietly with a straight-forward narrative about "Coach Jones." Coach Jones, he tells the players, had been a legendary head coach for the local high school, winning several state championships. Years passed, and Coach Jones retired and was succeeded by one of his former players. Under the new coach, the team did well initially, 8-2, 7-3, a few trips to the playoffs, but they never returned to the state championship game. Slowly, the team slipped to .500 seasons and then even lower. The town and players grew dissatisfied with the new head coach who was hounded by his own feelings of disappointment and frustration. Meanwhile, Coach Jones, who lived across the street from the practice field, watched the drama play out from a comfortable lawn chair. Ogilvie continues with the story.

"For a while, the new coach was too embarrassed to ask Coach Jones for help, but soon the pressure became too much. 'Coach Jones,' he said, 'I do everything you did.

49

We practice the same, we play the same system, we work just as hard, but we're not winning. What can I do?'

"'Do you really want to know?' Coach Jones asked.

"'Yes, please tell me. I'll do whatever it takes to start winning again.'

"'Then follow me.'

"Coach Jones led the new coach into the woods behind his house. The two men trudged through dark forest for nearly a mile to a point where the new coach feared getting lost. Soon they arrived at the edge of a pond, but Coach Jones kept on walking straight into the pond. The new coach hesitated as the old man pushed ahead until the water was waist high. The new coach wondered if old Coach Jones had gone senile.

"Coach Jones turned around and asked again, 'Do you really want to know what it takes to win state championships?'

"The new coach knew the correct answer would be to walk into the pond himself, and he did. He could feel the muck and slime in his shoes as he waded out to where Coach Jones was standing.

"Coach Jones asked again, 'Do you really want to know what it takes to win state championships?'

"'Yes, Coach Jones, I do.'

"Well, Coach Jones grabs the new coach and pushes his head beneath the water!"

Simultaneously, Ogilvie reaches toward an assistant coach standing nearby, and yanks his head down forcefully as if he's doing the same.

50

"The new coach is confused! At first he doesn't fight Coach Jones, but then 30 seconds pass, 45 seconds, one minute, and he's nearly out of breath! Horrible thoughts race through the new coach's mind. 'Is Coach Jones trying to kill me?' Finally, the new coach can't stay under any longer and he forces himself free from Coach Jones's grip."

Ogilvie releases the assistant coach.

"As the new coach sputters and gasps for air, Coach Jones looks him dead in the eye and says, 'When you want to win like you want that next breath of air ... that's when you'll win state championships! That's when you'll win state championships!'"

It's a small bit of motivational theater, and it works to the effect of shaking a can of pop. The players respond, howling with mania. The locker room door flies open, and the players pour out, some of them getting jammed side by side in the door frame, their shoulder pads too large to pass.

Led by the team captains, the team resumes an orderly jog and moves toward the field two-by-two, some of the players injecting extra hops and whoops into their stride. Assembling near the fence gate, the order breaks down, and the team morphs into a percolating mass of energy: their helmets resemble air bubbles escaping from a pot of boiling water. The crowd comes to its feet, clapping hands, shaking pom-poms, and holding home-made signs overhead. The band fires up like a jukebox with a new quarter. The clock has struck 7:30.

51

52

The cheerleaders toddle forward with a heavy and oversized painted sign that expands across the team's bulk. At the captains' signal, the players rush forward, breaking through the sign like a huge burst of light into a dark room, filling the vacuum on the field, delivering significance to this gathering, providing a focal point for the next two-and-a-half hours, and bearing the emotions and sense of wellness for so many town folk.

This spectacle. Why have you come? It would be hard to say at this point. Except that you wouldn't be anywhere else right now. You don't know anyone here. At least not yet. Even so, watching the players pile atop each other on the sidelines in front of you accompanied by the band's football soundtrack, you feel like you've stepped into your home. Now, about that seat ...

51. Struthers at Niles McKinley, 10/11/01

52. Avon Lake at Amherst Steele, 10/12/01

53. Avon Lake at Amherst Steele, 10/12/01

54. Mogadore v. Maria Stein Marion Local,
    Paul Brown Tiger Stadium, 12/1/01

54

PREGAME

55

55. Ashtabula Edgewood at
Hanoverton United, 8/25/01

56. Newcomerstown at
Bowerston Conotton Valley, 10/20/01

57. Lorain Southview at Shaker Heights, 10/13/01

58. Hamilton Badin v. Akron Manchester,
Virgil M. Schwarm Stadium, 9/8/01

56

THE WRITER Samuel Johnson once wrote, "Second marriages are the triumph of hope over experience." If Mr. Johnson had lived just another 100 years, and actually witnessed modern sport, he might have added football fans to that list of unreasonably optimistic souls who forbear in the midst of hard, contrary facts. Take a quick survey of the people sitting around you. Go ahead. Ask the woman with her hair dyed bright red, wearing the number 60 jersey and shaking a plastic pop bottle filled with popcorn kernels. Her team went 2-8 last season and graduated 17 starters in the off-season. What does she think about this year? *Oh, I think if the boys really work hard, they can be 8 and 2 this year. I read in the paper that this will be another building year. I just don't agree with that. Maybe this team doesn't have a lot of experience, but they've been practicing real hard this summer. That's just what I think.* Talk to the older fellow with the Davey Tree baseball cap who, in just the first few minutes of the game, has already twisted his program into a worried snarl of ink and tattered pages. His team finished an uninspired 5 and 5 last year when they lost to every team they played with a better record, and defeated four teams with a combined win total of ten games. In the off-season, the returning first-string quarterback broke his leg in three places while water skiing. He won't have the pins taken out of his leg until mid-October. *Yeah, I'd be real surprised if we didn't make the playoffs. We won five games last year and a lot of the teams in our conference will be weaker this season. In fact, I think if everything goes well — and I don't see why it shouldn't — we could probably make the regional finals.* Middling talent, poor coaching, young rubes,

57

FIRSTQUARTER

strong opponents — none of these appears particularly relevant when fans make their pre-season assessments.

And why should they, really? Underneath these sultry days of fading August, how could they feel any different about the chance for success? Sitting here in the stands, you feel the setting sun warming your face; your clothes are light, loose, and comfortable, and yet you feel it coming — that feeling of school approaching and the end to your long days of revelry and late weekday nights with friends. Yes, you may be several years away from

59

those textbook times, but when the days start losing light and the winds from the north blow a little drier, you succumb to that general malaise of autumn turn winter, turn cold, turn dark, turn winter some more. Your weekends become less adventurous. Nights are spent inside with family and friends, watching television, playing on the computer, and talking on the phone. There seems to be less time to fit in social events, so you schedule them carefully, needing the plans to get you out of the house. And, in that way, the football team and Friday night fill a unique role: They provide you with that hope, that optimism, that spark and potential for excitement you can carry through the slower months until spring inspires you to the outside world again.

Ed Mignery, the physically imposing yet genial head coach of Hamilton's Big Blue in southwestern Ohio, understands this need for Friday night games in the fall. In fact, he believes it's a principal reason for football's popularity. "Football has great structure. On

60

61

Tuesday, everywhere in the state, seventh grade plays. Wednesday, eighth grade. Thursday, ninth grade. Friday night belongs to high school varsity football. Saturday morning, reserves [and junior varsity] play. Saturday afternoon belongs to college football. Sunday belongs to pro football. It's so structured, and people know where they're going and when. Other sports play Tuesday, Wednesday, Saturday, Sunday, and people ask, 'Well, when do you play?' And we know in Ohio that [football's] so structured that people get ready for one game a week, and they look forward to it, and they know what's going on, and they set time aside for it."

Mignery, you quickly learn, is one of the more engaging spokesmen for the game. You imagine him talking X's and O's with fishing buddies into the late hours, hashing out plays and strategies and laughing over tall tales told countless times. He radiates enthusiasm with each point, speaks with conviction about all the facets of coaching and the potential of football to create better people, productive citizens, and reliable co-workers. At Hamilton, the largest high school in the state, Mignery has 80 players in his charge, a situation that provides too few playing minutes for too many players. But he doesn't worry about that. When players come out to practice each day, Mignery wants to see kids find the courage to make fast contact and the social skills to get along with the other 79. That's what football can teach.

The portal comes to life with the night's opening scene from Poland in Northeast Ohio. It's week one in late August, and hope is everywhere. The bleacher buzz returns. A soft hum at first. The kickoff team for Poland Seminary lines up along the 40 with their kicker, Shawn O'Halloran, five yards back, his arm raised, one finger pointing in the air.

59. Piqua at Troy, 9/21/01   60. Bellaire v. Richmond Edison, Nelson Field, 9/29/01   61. Piqua Band, Piqua at Troy, 9/21/01   62. Piqua at Troy, 9/21/01

On the other side of the field, the Tigers from New Middletown Springfield are spread evenly from sideline to sideline. As your view moves from the front ranks on the 50 to the last player standing near the end zone, you notice a gradual diminishment in size, the bears up front, the guys with thick limbs and plenty of deep grooves in the front of their helmets. Toward the back the numbers shrink and so do the appendages. These guys are lithe and smaller, and even if you haven't seen them take a step yet, you know they're quick. They hop up and down trying to stay loose and limber, waiting for that oblong orb to come falling out of the sky, bringing with it a ground-shaking tumult of heavy footfalls bearing down relentlessly on a single point: the guy with the ball.

The crowd rises to its feet. Cheerleaders twirl their megaphones overhead. Team mascots jangle their arms wildly in front of the crowd, trying to elicit more audible team support. The student section strikes up a low cheer: ahhhhhhhhhHHHHHHH! In a flash, O'Halloran thrusts his foot forward and everyone looks skyward. The ball traces an arc through the stadium down to the waiting arms of Springfield's Dan Zitkovic, standing with one foot poised behind him for instant locomotion once the ball feels securely in his grasp.

When you think about it, it's almost foolish — the way your heart rises to this moment. You've watched hundreds of kickoffs in your lifetime, and still you can't repress that surge of emotion when the game launches into action. Around you, the pressure and anticipation lift, shoulders relax, and you hear some laughter a couple rows up. Now you feel as if you're seeing the people in the stands for the first time, actually seeing who they are, this motley assemblage.

63

63. Kenton v. Newark Licking Valley, Canton Fawcett Stadium, 12/1/01

64. Cincinnati St. Xavier v. Cleveland St. Ignatius, Canton Fawcett Stadium, 12/1/01

65. Bellaire v. Richmond Edison, Nelson Field, 9/29/01

The spectators have settled into their seats, many of them hustling to regular spots. Others came to the field that morning and some the day before, to tape blankets down to the benches, a high school football stadium's version of squatter's rights, a practice that some schools have tried to discourage. Of course, some stadiums now feature reserve seating, but most have old-fashioned democratic general admission where it's first come, first served. The best seats go to the swift, the decisive, and those with shortened Friday work hours. But even general admission seating has unspoken but very established and respected zones. Like pews in church. Look up high, along the back row, just to the right of the press box. Shirley Hudson of Troy has been sitting there for 34 years, and in that span she's only missed a handful of games: one to have a baby, another due to medical emergency, and a third because she was out of the country. Of course, she still called international long distance to find out who won. You imagine that she must have acquired this devotion by watching her sons play for the Trojans, but your guess is off the mark. Hudson has only daughters. She says she likes the back row because she can whoop and cheer without obstructing anyone's view. Her husband prefers a closer view as he's worked on the Troy Memorial Stadium chain crew for over 30 years. Even at away games they stay far apart: he heads to the sidelines while Shirley makes the long trek up the stairs to the top row where she can recline, chat with friends, and take in the whole scene. "I just love football. I can't explain it," she says. The Hudsons can't conceive of a fall without Troy football, but when the day comes, "God forbid," Shirley's husband says, "I plan on buying her seat and roping it off."

> "WE DON'T HAVE THE OPERA IN FOSTORIA. FRIDAY NIGHT FOOTBALL IS OUR PASTIME."
>
> Donene Smith,
> Athletic Director, St. Wendelin H.S.

64

65

Meanwhile at the 50-yard line, about halfway up, you spot Marshall McCorkle from Bellaire wearing a baseball hat and red windbreaker. While the fans crammed into every space available tonight, no one dared take this spot. It belongs to Marshall, and he's earned it. At the youthful age of 85, Marshall has been a fixture at Big Red games since 1923, and to prove it he can rattle off the modes of transportation he's used to get to Nelson Field in downtown Bellaire: horse and buggy, streetcar, train, ferry, bus, automobile, and foot. In his younger days, Marshall preferred hanging along the fence where he could talk to the players and greet people coming into the stadium, a chance to catch up on the week's events with a quick word or two. Weakened legs, however, have forced him to take a seat in the stands, which will do for now. He'd go anywhere to watch Bellaire and Ohio Valley players. One Friday night, many years ago, on a weekend when Bellaire did not have a game scheduled, McCorkle's Dad proposed driving down to Durham, North Carolina, to watch two former Valley players then in college. By daybreak the next morning, the two men had already put a couple hundred miles behind them. McCorkle laughs heartily when he tells you this, perhaps astounded by his own devotion.

Interestingly, Marshall's loyalty did not come from his memories of playing. The McCorkle family ran a farm, and family duties kept young Marshall from donning the leather helmet and pads. Even if he had the time, he says he couldn't have played because they lived so far out in the country and there wouldn't have been any way for him to get home after practice. No, you would have to conclude that Marshall's loyalty was handed down like eye color, height, and build — through genetics. McCorkle's father attended Bellaire games until he was 95. In fact, one weekend, when the elder

66

67

McCorkle's health had begun to worsen, his mother asked Marshall to lie about Bellaire having a home game that week. Her son dutifully complied. His Dad said, "No matter. St. John's will be playing" (the local Catholic school that also uses Nelson Field), and rose to leave the house. Marshall quickly improvised, and told his Dad that he couldn't take him to the game because he had business of his own that afternoon. Seemingly the case was settled, and Marshall went to the game himself. Midway through the first quarter, to Marshall's utter astonishment, the elder McCorkle wandered in through the ticket gates, having walked two miles to the stadium. Tonight, the 50-yard line belongs to a McCorkle.

68

You watch the players scrum on the field for a few plays. They move freely and without hesitation now, confident of direction and purpose. That first contact, the feel of counter-force against theirs, has drained the nervousness into the turf beneath them. On defense, linemen shoot the gaps and stunt, forming a collective bulls' rush on their offensive counterparts. Linebackers fill the holes, human bottle stoppers, bracing for contact, shoving oncoming blockers aside, and breaking into fevered pursuit. Cornerbacks and safeties read, retreat, start, stop, and hustle, trying to shed pesky blockers who shadow them across the field. On the other side of the scrimmage line, offensive linemen hurtle themselves forward thanklessly again and again, pushing toward the goal line, hoping to withstand the surging rush long enough for the play to pass them by. Receivers check their position with the side judges and try to break free, running routes with dancer-like precision,

69

66. Member of chain crew, Mentor Lake Catholic v. Columbus St. Francis DeSales, Paul Brown Tiger Stadium, 11/30/01

67. Painesville Riverside at Columbus St. Francis DeSales, 9/15/01

68. Delphos Jefferson v. Ada, Delphos Stadium Park, 9/22/01

69. Kenton v. Newark Licking Valley, Canton Fawcett Stadium, 12/1/01

sharp, sudden breaks in direction, looking for the ball while trying to sense defenders swirling around them unseen, lying in guerilla wait for the moment they touch the ball. Running backs give themselves over to instinct, taking the handoff and letting their eyes and feet make all the decisions in split-second increments — whether to cut to the outside or duck through a hole or lower a shoulder into a rapidly approaching defender. It's all about finding free space.

"IN FACT, IF YOU LOOK
AROUND, YOU'LL SEE
OTHER COLLEGES
COMING INTO OHIO,
LIKE MICHIGAN, LIKE
INDIANA, FLORIDA,
AND PENN STATE.
THEY COME INTO OHIO
AND THEY WANT TO
TAKE OUR BOYS."

Tom Redmon,
Statistician, Portsmouth H.S.

For some of these fans, the game they watch today, for good or for bad, doesn't match the game they once played. The players are bigger, faster, stronger, yes — nearly everyone agrees on that — but the style of play has changed. During the celebrated tenure of Woody Hayes at Ohio State, "three yards and cloud of dust" became a statewide mantra for high school offensive coordinators. Relying on flawless execution, coaches assembled ranks of the biggest linemen they could find with strapping, fast running backs to plow through the holes, driving themselves forward for that magic four yards. But today, more teams are opening up with passing games, pro sets, and the occasional no-huddle, spread offense. Defenses run complex blitzing schemes and show multiple defensive fronts designed to unnerve the opposition. Coaches signal plays from the sidelines using fully-realized alphabets of hand gestures. The game has become more technical, due in large part to the increased exposure the media have given football. While televised games were formerly consigned to Saturday and Sunday afternoons, now young men can watch games throughout the week, at night, in the morning, replays on ESPN, Fox Sports Net, and local cable

70

70. Columbus Bishop Watterson v. Lexington, Mt. Vernon Yellow Jacket Stadium, 11/9/01

71. Fostoria St. Wendelin v. Oregon Cardinal Stritch, Fostoria Stadium, 9/1/01

72. Chesapeake Band, Crooksville at Chesapeake, 11/2/01

channels. Sports talk radio spews endless opinion about strategy, transactions, and possibility. For the ardent sports fan, today's world can truly be all sports, all the time. Has this changed the game? Not everyone thinks so.

An older gentleman sitting next to you — Albert Hobar — nudges an elbow into your side. "I know what you're thinking," he says, keeping a steady gaze on the field. "All that new stuff... it's just fluff. Basically the game is the same: you gotta pass, you gotta run, you gotta tackle." When Albert Hobar played football, fewer than 2,000 people lived in his Lake Erie shore hometown of Avon Lake. When Hobar entered Avon Lake High School in 1947, the game was six-man football, a version modified for smaller communities that couldn't field a full eleven. When Hobar buckled up his helmet for the Shoremen, the gridiron was 80 yards long, you needed 15 yards for a first down, and extra points were worth two if you drop-kicked the ball. When Hobar was a senior, his team went 19-2. When Hobar's team ran off straight victories over neighboring six-man teams from Avon, North Ridgeville, Sheffield Lake, and Grafton, conference opponents defined the borders of his sporting world. When Hobar's sons played for Avon Lake, he thinks they learned to get along with others in ways he couldn't teach. When Avon Lake squared off in 2001 against Amherst in a regular season meeting of the state's top-ranked teams in Division 2, he couldn't remember a more exciting day in the town's history (a game eventually won by the Shoremen). When the day comes that Hobar can't walk, that's when he'll stop going to Avon Lake games.

You think about Albert for a minute. He's right. The essence of the game is unchanged. All the innovations in the world can't change that fact. Running, passing, blocking,

71

72

tackling, and moving the ball toward your opponent's end zone — simple, basic concepts, like addition in math — are the base from which all other ideas spring.

As if to underscore the point, Windham's Tony Marstiller breaks a short run up the sidelines following on the tail of Josh Garrett, a senior guard who has pulled outside to lead this convoy. It began as a simple sweep to the right, everyone held their blocks, Garrett provided the moving interference out front, and Marstiller pushed to the outside. An eight-yard pick-up, and a fresh set of downs for the Division 5 Bombers. The crowd responds joyously.

73

Now you're watching plays from a week one match-up between the Bombers of Windham and the Wildcats of Southington Chalker, a rural school in Northeast Ohio named for Newton Chalker, a Civil War hero who settled the Southington area in the late 1800s. Both squads entered the 2001 season with good reason to expect post-season play. Windham made the playoffs the past two seasons, and returned several key starters at skill positions. Southington Chalker, meanwhile, was re-energized behind head coach Bill Ledsome, who led the Wildcats to the first three winning seasons in school history. This year, Ledsome had 12 returning lettermen, six on offense, and six on defense. Definitely a recipe for hope.

By the time Windham and Southington Chalker emerge through the gridiron portal (thus replacing Poland Seminary and New Middletown Springfield), the Bombers had already staked a 21-0 lead, and were threatening to score again. On the Wildcat

74

sidelines, Ledsome bites his lip and strokes his chin worriedly, due not so much to the current deficit (Windham is a division higher than Chalker), but for the possible long-term impact a first-game drubbing could inflict on his players. How many teams never recover from first-week routs? These are kids, and as eager as they are to strap up the Riddell, they sometimes lack the mental wherewithal to recover from early embarrassment. That's where coaching and motivation come in.

Zack Burns, senior quarterback for Windham, drops back to pass. Standing tall behind a wall of yellow helmets, he has plenty of time to scan the field. Tight end Adam Rogers drifts off the line and floats into the left side of the end zone. The Wildcats, in their home black uniforms with orange numbers, close on Burns, but he gets the ball away quickly. It's a tight spiral with plenty of zip, and Rogers hauls it in easily.

Touchdown. Paydirt. Score. Six. The House. Cheerleaders respond with jumps and acrobatic tumbling runs, players storm up and down the sidelines exchanging hugs and high-fives, the band blurts out an energized song, and confetti rains down on your head. The Windham touchdown has set the crowd abuzz on both sides of the field as the spectators turn to each other to share in the immediate mirth or distress.

Chalker will end up losing this game 48-12, but Ledsome will rally his team. They will win the last four games of the regular season to finish 6-3, and advance to the playoffs for the first time ever. And even though the Wildcats will bow out in the first round to a talented Tiffin Calvert team, they have experience now, something to build on, something to motivate the younger players, and something the team faithful can nurture in

75

73. Kenton v. Newark Licking Valley,
Canton Fawcett Stadium, 12/1/01

74. Windham at Southington Chalker, 8/25/01

75. Lincoln West v. Cleveland East,
Patrick Henry Field, 10/12/01

their hearts until next season. *We made the playoffs!* Windham, meanwhile, will narrowly miss a third straight playoff appearance, posting a 6-4 record, which included three straight defeats to end the season. Bomber fans will carry the bitter taste of near miss for a year, allowing it to fester, and provide a different strain of motivation.

"THERE'S NOT A WHOLE LOT OF THINGS IN YOUR NORMAL, EVERY DAY LIFE OR WORK WHERE YOU CAN GET THIS EXCITED ABOUT SOMETHING. FOR THE LAST 15 YEARS [AS A COACH], I'VE LIVED FOR THE FRIDAY NIGHTS. I CAN'T PLAY ANYMORE, BUT I CAN STILL COACH AND FEEL THAT THRILL OF COMPETITION."

Mike Fell,
Head Coach, Celina H.S.

On the sidelines, an older gentleman points an instamatic camera at another set of players as they hustle off the field. Between pictures, he shouts words of encouragement, calling each player by name, commiserating with their frustration, hoping his cheers will buoy the players' outlook, at least until they can find their own success. Most of the players keep their heads down, lost in tired disappointment, but one young man responds, "Thanks, Digger."

Frank "Digger" Dawson from East Liverpool is a mortician and frankly, when you meet him, you can't imagine a less likely candidate for the job. His constant good spirits and enjoyment of being around friends belie the somber mood you would expect for someone whose daily work consists of helping family members say goodbye to loved ones. In his silvery late 60s, Digger shakes hands at football games the way politicians work the crowds at county fairs. He knows virtually everyone in town, and their parents and grandparents, too. Send a letter to Digger in East Liverpool. Forget the address. Just mark it "Digger Dawson." It will get into his hands.

76

WILDCAT FANS

76. Windham at Southington Chalker, 8/25/01

77. Mogadore v. Maria Stein Marion Local, Paul Brown Tiger Stadium, 12/1/01

Digger doubles as the Potters' team historian and curator of the Ohio Valley Hall of Fame. His opus work, *We Are the Potters*, chronicles a century of East Liverpool football, charting the evolution of this industrial city, from the boom of the pottery industry to the subsequent lean times when those businesses moved elsewhere for less expensive labor. To Digger, the recent history of East Liverpool can be told in relation to Potter football, and in relation to particular families — such as the Griffins or Bells — who have sent multiple generations through the program. East Liverpool can be understood through its football coaches — Wade Watts, Bob McNea, and Bob Thayer, to name just a few — who have trained legions of young men to go forth and carry the pride of East Liverpool to the whole wide world. East Liverpool is also explained by native sons like Lou Holtz, who overcame great odds to become a legendary football figure. "When the town needs something," Digger says, "it's the football people who step up and give and lead. If I ever got in trouble, I know where I could find a lot of ex-Potters who would help me out. That's been my experience."

If you travel south on State Route 11 toward East Liverpool, somewhere between Leetonia and Lisbon, in the months before the hoary breaths of winter turn the land gray, brown, and white, you can see dazzling pumpkin patches along either side of the road. The view helps you envision items of comfort: padded chairs, roaring fires, and thick sweaters. The placid and spectacular view makes it hard to imagine that towns and rivalries in this area have avoided playing each other for years on end due to safety concerns. In 1965, a brawl between Steubenville and East Liverpool caused school officials to ban that matchup until tempers simmered down and a small degree of amnesia settled in. Even if you have never been involved in this kind of fracas or inter-city antagonism, you sort of

understand it. You understand how, in the name of a football team, perfect strangers in town became true comrades in the stadium. You've at least felt those impulses, the burgeoning pride that fills you at once with strength and protective fear. On one hand, *the town is behind you. We are united.* And on the other, *what if we lose?* That pride in your team, that awesome, unexamined power — it doesn't *always* bring out our best. We acknowledge this and hopefully we learn from it.

The Steubenville-East Liverpool incident has been long buried and replaced by a renewed rivalry, centering around a much-anticipated game that, as of late, tends to have playoff implications. East Liverpool hasn't won in Steubenville since 1964, and if you've been to Harding Stadium and stood on the visiting team's meager sidelines beneath the fire-breathing stallion on the scoreboard, you understand why winning there is a difficult thing to do.

Now if you find yourself in Steubenville, don't go asking about Steubenville's high school football team. It's *Big Red* football. And if you've been a long-time fan, you say, *I've been watching Big Red since I was a kid.* And if you're planning to hit Harding Stadium that evening, you proclaim proudly, *I'm going to see Big Red play tonight!* And if you missed the game due to an emergency appendectomy (which would be one of the few acceptable reasons to miss a game) you ask, *How'd Big Red do tonight?*

If you want to know how Big Red did on any given night, Joe Heatherington would be your best bet for a reliable answer. Back in 1932, young Joe would race home from school, toss his books inside the front door, and take a seat on his family's front porch.

Minutes later, Big Red players would file past, cleats strung around their necks, making the long trek up North Fifth Street from the high school downtown to the stadium for practice. When Heatherington finished his military service in 1946, he returned to Steubenville and bought season tickets to Big Red football, but sitting in the stands to support his hometown team wasn't good enough for him. Heatherington enlisted as the equipment manager, and for the next 25 years he traveled far and wide with Big Red until open-heart surgery forced him to cut back his duties. One evening, shortly after that surgery, Heatherington's nurse maneuvered Joe's bed next to his hospital room window. Although puzzled by her action, he had no questions, only tears, when he looked down and saw head coach Reno Saccoccia and Big Red lined up across the hospital lawn to wish him a speedy recovery.

79

On that day when Saccoccia gathered his team beneath the hospital window, he might have felt he owed Heatherington gratitude for reasons greater than his services as equipment manager. You see, Heatherington's wife literally brought Saccoccia into this world. As the nurse in his delivery room, she gave the Steubenville head coach that first cry-slash-oxygen-inducing slap on the bum. Could she have known at that time what that slap would mean for Steubenville? As she wrapped the infant Saccoccia in a warm blanket, could she have imagined this mewling infant would become head coach in 1983 and lead Big Red to its first and only state title in 1984? As she sucked vestigial mucous from his tiny red nostrils, might she have foreseen, in a flashing

80

78. Hamilton Badin v. Akron Manchester,
    Virgil M. Schwarm Stadium, 9/8/01

79. Newcomerstown at Bowerston
    Conotton Valley, 10/20/01

80. Kenton v. Newark Licking Valley,
    Canton Fawcett Stadium, 12/1/01

vision, that Big Red would make 12 trips to the playoffs in 18 years under his guidance? Could she have known the depth of loyalty her husband would exhibit when he said he intends to be buried with his commemorative Big Red state title watch on his wrist? Probably not, but it would make a good story.

The Waverly Tigers and the Wellston Golden Rockets appear on the field now, two Division 4 squads from southern Ohio that feature high-octane offenses with big play capacity. Waverly relies on the strong arm of quarterback Jay Gullion and the quick feet

of running back Zach Montavan, who gained over 1,600 yards as a junior. Wellston, meanwhile, knows its success will depend largely on senior tailback Brad Young, who picked up 1,868 yards and notched 26 touchdowns in his junior year.

Many fans thought this game might foreshadow a post-season rematch. Before four minutes had elapsed in the first quarter, Waverly and Wellston exchanged touchdowns; however, neither one of them came on the ground. In fact, Montavon would not get in the end zone during this game, despite gaining over 100 yards. Young, for his part, was kept in check by the Tigers for most of the first half (a 91-yard kickoff return notwithstanding), managing only a series of short runs. In the second half — the scene you're watching now — he picks up momentum, notching three scores, the last coming with just 1:47 left in the game, giving the Golden Rockets a 30-28 lead.

Down on the sidelines, head coach Ed Bolin, in his 18th and final year at Waverly, calmly paces the sidelines as his offense takes the field. The Tigers have the ball on their own 40-yard line with just over a minute and a half to play. You think Bolin might be concerned with this type of situation presenting itself so early in the season, before most teams have jelled. In week three, many teams are still looking for that team ideal, trying to remember plays, and getting the timing down. The pressure of a last-minute drive can shatter the resolve of professional players. What could a coach expect from a group of teenagers?

Whatever fears Bolin may have entertained on this humid September night, they have no effect on his Tiger offense. With their gold helmets shining beneath the stadium lights, you stare in amazement as quarterback Jay Gullion completes his first two throws for 42 yards. Just like that, the Tigers have a first and ten on Wellston's 18-yard line. On the next play, 270-pound center Josh Lowe leads his team up to the line and fires the snap to Gullion, who takes a five-yard drop. Creed Miller, the lanky two-way player who snuffed a Wellston drive in the first half with an interception, bolts into the end zone. Gullion lays the ball up softly, allowing Miller to utilize his height advantage. The junior split end pulls it down for the winning score. Behind you, a man exclaims, his hands pressed against the sides of his head, *Can you believe it!?* As you watch the Tigers rejoice on the sidelines, you figure it's a question for which an answer does not matter.

> "WHERE ELSE CAN YOU CHEER FOR 11 GUYS AT ONE TIME? ALL THE OTHER SPORTS LET FEWER KIDS PLAY."
>
> Kim Schaber, Parent,
> Woodsfield Monroe Central H.S.

84

81. Lorain Southview at
    Shaker Heights, 10/13/01

82. Lakewood St. Edward v.
    Cleveland St. Ignatius,
    Lakewood Stadium, 10/13/01

83. Mentor Lake Catholic v.
    Columbus St. Francis DeSales,
    Paul Brown Tiger Stadium, 11/30/01

84. Kenton v. Newark Licking Valley,
    Canton Fawcett Stadium, 12/1/01

Watching this assortment of players from around Ohio, you are impressed by the level of participation in the state. From the junior leagues to the college level, it seems you can't travel ten miles in any direction without coming across a football game, whether it's a sanctioned game with officials and chain crews, or a ragtag group throwing wobbly Nerf spirals around an open field. In the Saturday morning sports section of the paper, look beneath the scores from your area in the section marked "Around Ohio." An expansive list unfolds, many of the items reporting teams and results from towns you've never heard of, places like New Matamoras, Salineville,

85

Edgerton, and Mount Orab. Players, coaches, bands, cheerleaders, and fans just like you trudge to the stadium every weekend with ritual hopes and fears and the same desire for a capstone moment to the work week now passed. As Hamilton's Mignery said, we know when our teams play, and we plan for it.

With all this sameness, all these elements of the game that draw us together on weekends, it causes some amusement when regional factions speak up. Consider that every team wears the same style uniforms, executes the same plays, practices the same drills, learns the same fundamentals, and yet defenders for their particular brand of football are easy to find.

Head coach Jerry Buti has spent over 20 years coaching in Northwest Ohio, most recently at Defiance High School. "I think we play the best football in the state right here. I always tell our kids, the farther you go East, the less football you're

86

87

supposed to know." With state titles coming home to Northwest Ohio every year (St. Mary's Memorial, Archbold, and Toledo St. Francis DeSales, for example), Buti's point is well-taken.

Down in Cincinnati, Ohio, a 2001 *Cincinnati Enquirer* headline read, "Queen City? Football City!" a proclamation inspired by a *USA Today* high school football poll that ranked three area teams in its Super 25, an unprecedented achievement for any metropolitan area. The morning that headline ran, Colerain High School assistant coach Dan Scholz told you, "Don't believe what they say up there in the North. All those people up there say they're better and they're not."

88

A web site dedicated to the Midwest Athletic Conference in west central Ohio touts this collection of teams as "the #1 small school conference in Ohio." And, indeed, there is an extensive list of state titles residing among the members of this group. St. Henry's and Versailles, two towns less than 20 miles apart, have won nine state football titles collectively (four for St. Henry's and five for Versailles). Add Delphos St. John's, Maria Stein Marion Local, and Minster to this mix, and that number becomes 15.

In Northeast Ohio — Stark County to be exact — within the far-reaching shadows of the Pro Football Hall of Fame, two of the nation's winningest programs stand less than 20 minutes apart. With nearly 1,500 victories between them, Massillon Washington and

85. McComb v. Columbus Grove, Lima Stadium, 11/17/01

86. Avon Lake at Amherst Steele, 10/12/01

87. Painesville Riverside at Columbus St. Francis Desales, 9/15/01

88. Bedford St. Peter Chanel, 11/23/01

Canton McKinley have been virtual symbols for high school football excellence. When these teams met for the 100th straight year in 1994, no less than ESPN and *Sports Illustrated* provided coverage of the game to a national audience.

Ohio Valley fields, stretching 300 miles from Youngstown to Portsmouth, have proven a consistent source of college and professional talent, producing players and coaches with names like Lou Groza, Bob Stoops, and Joey Galloway. A season cannot pass you by without seeing an Ohio Valley player on television, performing in front of a national audience.

But if the names and records weren't famous, and if no magazine had ever bothered to write about football in your town, you'd probably still be here, in the stands, leafing through the glossy pages of a program, eavesdropping on conversations four rows behind you, looking for your children gamboling on a small patch of grass in the corner the stadium, shifting your buttocks for relief on the hard bench seat, enjoying the mix of fragrances, the comforting hum of humanity, and hey, even the game. The sun has disappeared, and a noticeably cooler breeze moves across the field. The first quarter has ended.

89

90

91

89. Bedford St. Peter Chanel v. Marion Pleasant,
    Canton Fawcett Stadium, 11/30/01

90. Cincinnati St. Xavier v. Cleveland St. Ignatius,
    Canton Fawcett Stadium, 12/1/01

91. Lorain Southview at Shaker Heights, 10/13/01

92. Newcomerstown v. Bowerston Conotton
    Valley, 10/20/01

93

93. Kenton v. Newark Licking Valley,
    Canton Fawcett Stadium, 12/1/01

94. Toledo Woodward Band, Toledo Woodward
    at Toledo Libbey, 10/27/01

95. Mentor Lake Catholic v. Columbus St. Francis
    DeSales, Paul Brown Tiger Stadium, 11/30/01

96. Lincoln West v. Cleveland East, Patrick Henry
    Field, 10/12/01

94

ACROSS MANY FIELDS

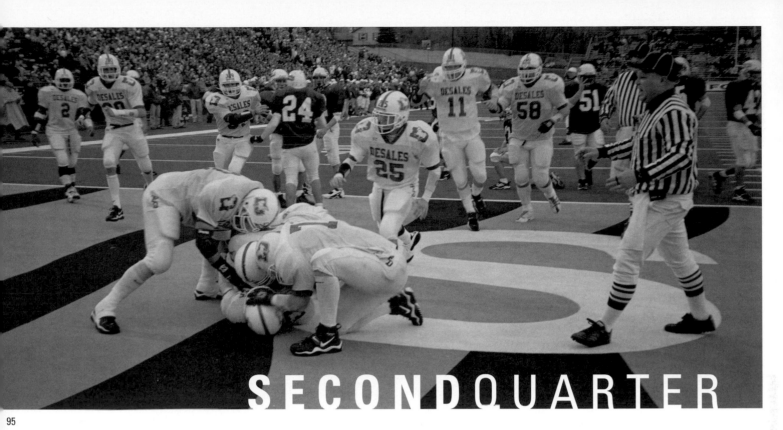

SECONDQUARTER

YOU overhear a nearby conversation.

What's the best game you ever saw? I mean the best game ever. And while you're thinking, hand me that program.

Long pause.

Wow. All right. 1996. Division six state final, Mogadore versus St. Henry's. Mogadore trails 35-9 at halftime. Second half they come out like banshees, like a guy trapped in a phone booth full of bees. Mogadore mounts a huge comeback. Chuck Moore breaks long touchdown runs. Scott Tompkins catches a 75-yard bomb and runs back an interception 60 yards for a score — both state championship game records! Mogadore wins 61-58. Three overtimes!

Naw, naw. Too high scoring. No defense. I'll take 1997: Germantown Valley View and Akron Manchester. State final game. Five overtimes! 31-24, Valley View. Their third state title. Everyone — players, fans — totally spent!

Wait a sec. Even better! 1986. Newark Catholic beats Defiance Ayersville 28-27. Newark Catholic drives the field in the last two minutes of the game like a pro squad, throwing out patterns, running out of bounds, saving the clock. You would have thought it was Joe Montana and the Niners. It was amazing.

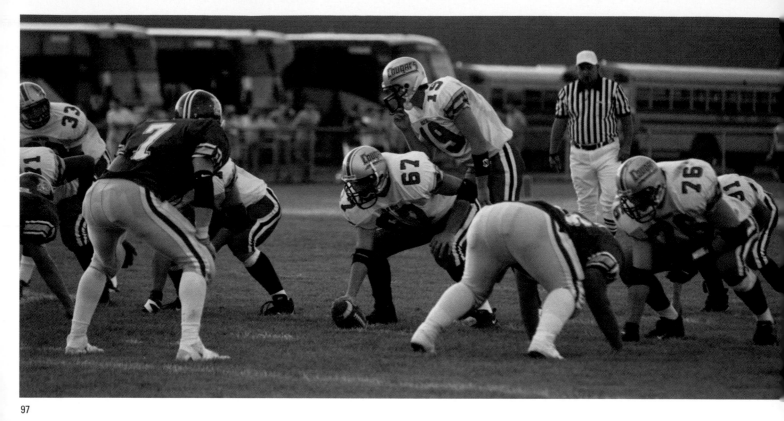

97

You listen to these two go back and forth like this for a couple of minutes. The games roll out one after another, mechanically, with a steadily increasing "sensational" quotient. Two things strike you. First is the emotion. They gesticulate madly while they speak, their eyes and facial expressions saying as much as their words. They speak without reservation, without fear that those sitting near them will see this excitement as strange or threatening or even ridiculous. No, it's football they're talking about — constant one-upsmanship and childlike exhilaration are completely acceptable. The second thing is the level of description. These same people, who might not be able to tell you what they had for lunch, can dredge up the minutest details about these games. The weather was cold with nimbus clouds and a northeasterly breeze, the ball sat on the 26-and-a-half-yard line, the coach substituted two interior line-man on the game's crucial play, the referee paused momentarily before starting the clock again, the quarterback's cousin's next door neighbor used to play running back for Gibsonburg who made the playoffs four years in row. Now you don't know how many of these details are "true" or "remembered as true," but it's the act of putting them together in brilliant rapid-fire succession that makes you step back and take note. Perhaps, one might argue, this long-term memory could be better devoted to something else, but that doesn't concern you tonight.

98

Asking certain Ohioans to share their thoughts on football is akin to asking an evangelical to share his or her thoughts on religion. The words come fast and fierce, with

99

97. Defiance v. Van Wert, Fred J. Brown Stadium, 8/31/01

98. Cincinnati Archbishop Moeller at Cincinnati Elder, 10/5/01

99. Toledo Woodward at Toledo Libbey, 10/27/01

no shortage of opinion or detail. The conversation starts with football, but invariably turns to other aspects of life, and then back to football, and then back to life again. Football is the ultimate icebreaker, a haven in which people can safely connect. When you're in line waiting to pay for gas, it might feel a bit odd to ask, *So, how're you doing tonight?* but perfectly comfortable to inquire, *So, you going to the game tonight?* And many times, you'll get the same answer. While the respondent might feel squeamish about replying to the first question, *Well, not too good. I think I got a touch of the flu,* he or she will feel less exposed in saying to the second *No, I'm a little under the weather. I'll have to read about it in the paper.* Not everyone in Ohio can tell you about the orchestra, or changes in the governor's budget, but even old Miss Marlow at the end of the street, who no one has seen in 15 years, whose house is now overgrown with untended shrubs and willow tree branches, knows a little something about the local team, even if it's just about the two intrepid band members who recently knocked on her door selling season tickets.

Three years ago, Columbus fireman John Ansell had a problem, a problem he sought to fix. Ansell's problem was high school football and how to get scores from around the state in an efficient manner. He subscribed to a Columbus paper, but understandably it reported area scores and devoted little room for games from Toledo, Cleveland, Cincinnati, and Youngstown. This Bishop Ready graduate had interests in games outside central Ohio. Ansell followed Harbin point rankings, he dreamed about post-season matchups, he compared teams with similar opponents, and he wanted to know more about the teams he'd be watching at the state championships later that season. More than anything, he wanted to meet other people who shared his addiction, a clandestine support group who, come Sunday morning, needed a comprehensive score fix.

100

101

In May 1999, Ansell posted a bulletin board on the Internet asking people to add game results from around the state. His initial vision was modest, hoping for a small community of dedicated fans who could be relied upon to report each weekend. By June, Ansell had a new problem. His tiny bulletin board was choking with hits, hundreds a day. He needed an upgrade. In July 1999, JJ Huddle (www.jjhuddle.com) was born, galvanizing Ohio's high school football community and officially sending it into information overdrive.

> "WE ARE CHRISTIANS,
> BUT WE ARE
> WARRIORS WHEN
> WE ARE ON THE FIELD,
> AND WE ARE ON THE
> FIELD TO WIN."
> Lisa Bradley, Athletic Director,
> World Harvest Christian Academy H.S.

Today, JJ Huddle has over 14,000 registered users and Ansell estimates another 14,000 view the site on a read-only basis. High schoolers around the state scurry to computer labs during free periods to find out the latest news about upcoming opponents. Typically responsible adults take frequent peeks to see what new topics (generated at nearly one a minute) have appeared since they took their last phone call. Registered users pick a name to conceal their identity and from there engage in high school football's largest electronic cocktail party. Head coach openings around the state? Ask on the Huddle. Want to know who's going to fill Jedediah Stephen's shoes at Sarahsville Shenandoah? Consult the Huddle. What's a good 40 time for an offensive tackle? Someone on the Huddle will tell you. How would the 1961 Niles McKinley team fare against Cincinnati Purcell-Marian's 1986 squad? Try it out on the Huddle. Does anyone remember Fred Jones? He might have played for Smithville in the 1970s, or it might've been Rittman? The Huddle will furnish an answer.

100. Lakewood St. Edward v. Cleveland St. Ignatius, Lakewood Stadium, 10/13/01

101. Crooksville at Chesapeake, 11/2/01

102. Lincoln West v. Cleveland East, Patrick Henry Field, 10/12/01

102

But don't go thinking you can just post anything you like. The Huddle has a strict code of decorum. If you want to talk smack, this is not the place. If you want to start rumors in a feeble attempt to rile your opponent or play head games, you'll be contacted promptly. Huddlers with names like Zanes-Vegas, Cats44, and Panama Jack keep vigilant patrol on the Huddle, preserving institutional congeniality. If you're posting "skunk," they'll call you on it and give you a quick "gong" from the group.

And so Ansell has moved forward, staying with the Huddle and branching out into new media. He co-hosts a weekly radio show in Columbus and writes a regular column for a newspaper in Mansfield. He never imagined his concept would grow as it has. He's pleased for the success of the Huddle. It keeps his addiction satisfied and thriving. But more than that, Ansell loves his fellow Huddlers. His use of the Internet has brought Ohio's high school football community into cyberspace, thousands of willing conversationalists now literally mouse clicks away.

Tom Mullen, Brian Bill, and Phil Heil met each other on the Huddle. They exchanged e-mails and met for dinner before games. None of this would be particularly interesting unless you knew they all graduated from Cincinnati Elder and yet did not know each other from their school years. They found each other extolling and defending the virtues of Panther football on the Huddle and other football web sites. Pretty soon, they started hosting out-of-town Huddlers from opposing teams — Cleveland St. Ignatius, Warren Harding — by treating them to drinks at the Kohlhaus and three-way chilis at Price Hill Chili. Then the visitors watch their teams receive a thorough whipping in "The Pit," one of USA Today's top-ten high school stadiums in the country, a most unfriendly confines

103. Mentor Lake Catholic v. Columbus St. Francis DeSales, Paul Brown Tiger Stadium, 11/30/01

104. Toledo Woodward at Toldeo Libbey, 10/27/01

105. Circleville at Ashville Teays Valley, 9/14/01

103

where many a talented team has suffered ignominiously before a vocal crowd that at times seems barely inches from the field.

Between quarters, you excuse yourself from your row and trudge up to the top of the

stands where a rickety metal ladder with rusting bolts and crenellated rungs leads to the roof of the press box. There's a four-foot chain link fence running along the perimeter here, just enough barrier to keep the average person from taking an accidental dive into the crowd below, but sufficiently low to accommodate a bank of video cameras, their noses pointing curiously downward to the field. You sidle in and take in the view. It is, in a word, magnificent. For miles around, lights stipple the landscape, a thin band of darkening indigo sinks into the horizon, and above you, the stadium lights blaze. Illumination floods the field, the stands teem with motion and life, and you feel as if you can see the energy rising from the ground, shimmering like heat haze from a

104

sun-baked highway. The weather has grown colder. The shorts and t-shirts have been put away in favor of long pants, jeans, long sleeves, and light jackets. You lean over the rail to pick out individuals from the stands and imagine what their lives must be like, what their stories are, why they're sitting here tonight. What connects us? It couldn't just be football. No. You know that, sometimes, other things bring us here.

During the fourth week of the 2001 season, something terrible happened. Something that had not happened before. On a Tuesday morning, the unspeakable occured, and we

ACROSS MANY FIELDS

105

don't know how to talk about it. And so we sat in front of our televisions, watching with disbelief. We talked with friends on the telephone and walked around in a muffled daze, looking for explanations that would ultimately never satisfy. Then the weekend came, and talk surfaced about what we should do. Is it time to go outside again? Is it time to start moving past what happened? Is the time right to play football again? Whatever decision was reached was not without serious misgivings. In a situation like this, how can anyone be sure of the right thing to do? Nearly every high school in Ohio decided to play football, and for many of us who climbed into the stands on Friday and Saturday night, it was the first time since the horror of September 11 occurred that we were with each other again, shoulder to shoulder in the stands, shaking hands a little longer, watching our kids, listening to the band, trying to regenerate that notion of community, a term we use differently now, a term that has become richer in meaning.

Down in Ashville, at Teays Valley High School, week four featured a game against Circleville, the Vikings' most intense rival. Under normal circumstances, it would be the most anticipated game of the year, a rivalry fraught with fierce battles and annual practical jokes played at the opposing team's expense. A few years ago, after a Circleville win in Ashville, the Circleville players rang the Teays Valley bell, a sign of disrespect that could not and would not be taken lightly. That next week, some irate Vikings drove to Circleville and painted their victory bell Teays Valley blue and gold. This year, however, by the time Friday arrived, the players were less concerned about who they were playing, and the planned pranks were left undone.

126. Cincinnati St. Xavier v. Cleveland St. Ignatius, Canton Fawcett Stadium, 12/1/01

127. Lorain Southview at Shaker Heights, 10/13/01

128. Lakewood St. Edward v. Cleveland St. Ignatius, Lakewood Stadium, 10/13/01

126

acknowledge something in the game much bigger than himself or his teams. On a long post-season bus trip, when most teams watch movies like *Gladiator*, *Rocky*, and *Remember the Titans*, Clifford showed the documentary *Football in America*, wanting his players to appreciate the scope and the vast array of people in our country who attempt to take meaning from this straight-forward exercise of moving a ball toward your opponent's goal line. Just look at our city, Clifford points out. Long after the pottery, coal, and oil businesses have taken their dollars elsewhere, football has been Crooksville's constant, the place where the community can feel like a community again, full of frailty and imperfection, yes, but a community nonetheless.

As the halftime show assembles on the field, many fans remain on their feet, roused to a higher level of consciousness by this torrent of football action, endless teams and highlights, up and downs, lefts and rights. They turn to each other and talk about the first half, using their hands liberally to explain their version of what happened. Their faces are excited or disappointed, their responses full of delight or nagging agitation. And you? Well, you're just happy to be here among these people, amidst the collection of shared experience. You'll carry your own memories of the first half with you (Waverly's last minute drive, Ashburn's touchdown catch) and, many years from now, or maybe next week, those memories will be called forth to remind you of this moment when you stood at the top of the stands listening to the gentle whirr of fellowship and football.

128

SECOND QUARTER

129

129. Delphos Jefferson v. Ada, Delphos Stadium Park, 9/22/01

130. Troy Band, Piqua at Troy, 9/21/01

131. McComb v. Columbus Grove, 11/17/01

132. Badin Band, Hamilton Badin v. Akron Manchester, Virgil M. Schwarm Stadium, 9/8/01

YOU'RE hungry. Yeah, you're hungry. Because you got lost in town, you didn't have time to stop at that local diner for a barstool helping of meatloaf, roasted redskin potatoes, side salad with bleu cheese dressing, and lime Jell-O topped with imitation whipped cream. And that's what you would have eaten because it was the "house special" and the waitress would have assured you it was the best thing on the menu that night. But none of this happened because you got lost, and now you're faced with grabbing some quick fare from the concession stand — which isn't altogether a bad thing.

131

The smart people, at least in terms of getting food, left their seats with two minutes to go in the half. Yes, they missed Ashburn's touchdown for Niles McKinley, but now they're standing at the head of this serpentine line, minutes away from accessing a smorgasbord of Super Ropes, hot dogs, pizza, bottled soda (in the South), bottled pop (in the North), candy bars, coffee, hot chocolate, and popcorn. Depending on the location, you will find some unique additions to this list (funnel cakes, frozen lemonade, barbequed ribs, and chicken breast sandwiches, for example), but you can find any number of people dining on one of these staple items in nearly every stadium in the state. After you secure your purchase, it's on to the condiment table, which before the game was a tidy display of napkins, plastic eating utensils, cardboard carrying trays, and various relishes. Now it looks like the remains of a 15th century operating table: congealed ketchup and mustard spills, crumpled wads of wet paper, shallow pools of brown liquid, and a napkin dispenser that's either empty or has its

132

HALFTIME

contents bored so deeply inside that it would take the tiny fingers of a baby combined with the strength of the Incredible Hulk to pull out a single sheet. But no matter. You weren't expecting French cuisine. Just sustenance. Just enough to keep your energy high for the second half. And besides, you've just contributed to the band booster club. That tepid tube of meat and cereal filler you're going to order may enable one more flute player to attend band camp next summer. That 12-ounce Styrofoam cup of coffee will help finance the new equipment trailer needed to haul the band's kettle drum set and other instruments. That salty and (almost) stale popcorn will pay travel expenses for the

133

band's next trip to the state competition. Let's face it. It will be the tastiest meal you've had in weeks, but it's certainly not one that will earn you high marks from the local cardiologist. You tell yourself it's OK. It's for the kids.

As the line inches forward, you have a few minutes to consult your program. You were so busy moving around during the first half, you didn't even take a look at the rosters, the coaching staff bios, or the list of items you might buy with a school logo emblazoned on the surface: bean bag chairs, seat cushions, bar stools, towels, pillows, card tables, key fobs, hats, shirts, socks, sweatpants, ad infinitum. If you can't wait to obtain these items using the order forms provided in the program, you may be able to find what you need in the tent next to the concession stand where the Mother's Club has set up shop.

134

135

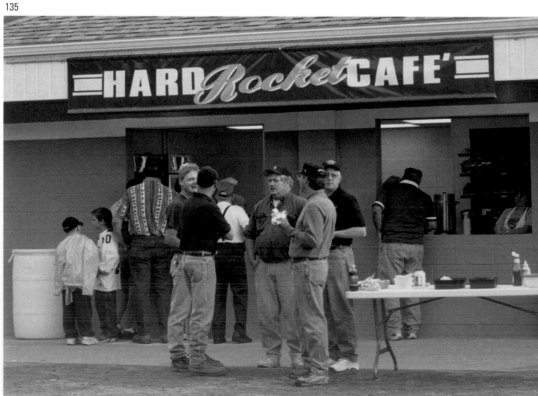

In colonial times, men would paint the family name on the sides of their water pails. This was one way to distinguish them from the many other pails at the local water pump, and to insure that they would not be stolen. When a house fire broke out somewhere in town, men would grab their pails and hustle to the scene to assist others in smothering the blaze. After the fire had been doused, the men would drop their pails right there and return home. The next day, the afflicted family would walk around town returning those pails to the rightful owners. In some ways, it was just a nice gesture and chance to say thank you to the men who helped out. It also served, however, as a way in which that family could take note of who had come to help when they needed it. *You helped us with our fire. We'll be sure to help you with yours.*

Programs serve a similar function, like public registries of who supports their team, how they support it, and how much. Consider the home program for the Crimson Tornadoes from Dover. They've been playing football since the late 1800s, and their rivalry with New Philadelphia is one of the state's oldest and most notable. By the sheer volume of supporters listed, it would appear that nearly everyone in Dover has purchased some room in the program. Some people buy advertisements for local businesses (*Goshen Dairy. Go Tornadoes! Visit us after the game!*) while others buy spirit squares where they can publish an inspirational message for their son, daughter, grandson, granddaughter, or maybe just a neighbor's child. Most people pledge enough to have their names printed in the directory of team supporters, the Tornado Patrons. Other high schools sell engraved bricks or plaque nameplates where a family or business can display its support in a special walkway or glass case somewhere within the stadium. It's an impressive outpouring of financial backing when you remember that these same

136

133. Men's Room, Alexander Stadium, Piqua, 9/21/01

134. Bo Rein Stadium, Niles McKinley H.S., 10/11/01

135. Paul Menichini Field, Lowellville, 8/23/01

136. Bellaire Band, Bellaire v. Richmond Edison, Nelson Field, 9/29/01

people likely reserve space in the winter sports program, attend booster functions, and regularly buy season tickets.

The proceeds are not treated lightly. Handling these precious dollars requires an implicit city-wide covenant to insure they will be distributed appropriately. As John Harris of Lexington said, sports programs run like a business and must never dip into the red. At Dover, the booster finances are public record like the earnings of a company on the stock market. The Tornado Club prints its ledger inside the front cover of the program: income and projects against expenses and donations. In 2000, the Tornado Club raised $100,000 and spent $105,000 — a slight deficit that was offset by a beginning balance of $45,000. The moneys were raised through a combination of social events and games of chance: Canal Days Booth ($4,303), Fish Fries ($6,881), golf scramble ($8,940), and a Harley raffle ($1,809). The fall and winter sports programs, like the one you're reading now, provided the largest source of income for the year ($18,930). On the expense side of the ledger, the Tornado Club allocated $14,459 for the football team and $95.80 for girls' tennis. It may look one-sided, and even sexist, but when you consider the equipment and event costs of a football game compared with a tennis match that brings in virtually no revenue, the injustice appears a little less unjust. Besides, an athletic director will tell you, a large portion of the tennis program is funded by football's gate receipts. It's safe to say the Tornadoes are in good shape: these booster funds will be pooled with tax dollars already earmarked for school extra-curriculars.

Not all communities have this luxury. Many towns without a large business base from which to draw public revenue face increasing pressure to raise property taxes or suffer pro-

137

137. United Band, Ashtabula Edgewood at Hanoverton United, 8/25/01

138. Struthers Band, Struthers at Niles McKinley, 10/11/01

139. Kenton Band, Kenton v. Coldwater, Findlay Donnell Stadium, 11/24/01

140. St. Xavier Band, Cincinnati St. Xavier v. Cleveland St. Ignatius, Canton Fawcett Stadium, 12/1/01

gram cuts within the school system. Sports, the school board officials are required to say, would be the first programs to go. We are, after all, an educational system.

Game programs aren't merely a reflection of a community's financial interest in its local team. They're also glossy-paged compendiums of town spirit, personal history, and civic values all boiled down to a shared interest in this football team, a collection of our sons and daughters who take the field — on the team and in the band — every weekend to represent us: *a random grouping of human beings still coming to know who we are, the public proper, the people of Town X.* Programs read as an extension of that football pride. Look at the names of the football record holders for your school. Yes, they're remarkable achievements, but every team has someone who's gained 1,000-plus yards, someone who's run back an interception 50 yards for a touchdown, and someone who's kicked three field goals in a game. You love those pages because of the names and the dates: the who, the when, and the against whom. They take you back to another time, another year, when you were younger, when you were different, and when you saw the world differently. You've changed a great deal since then, but one thing is still the same: Your team is down on that field still trying to win for the town. These records holders, these young men, you *knew* them. Or maybe you *remember* them. They're athletes produced in *your* town, athletes who thrilled the crowd with their ability and for a while gave everyone a chance to think of something good, something other than the hum-drum, work-a-day world they left behind earlier that day.

> "WE TAKE A LOT OF PRIDE IN WHAT WE DO. THE AUDIENCE HERE IN DEFIANCE EVERY WEEK EXPECTS US TO BE DOING A DIFFERENT SHOW. A GOOD SHOW AND AN ENTERTAINING SHOW.
>
> Vince Polce, Music Director, Defiance H.S.

138

139

140

Programs encourage good behavior, too. You've read this anonymous poem in many programs around the state:

Please don't curse that boy down there,
He is my son you see,
He's only just a boy, you know.
He means the world to me.

I did not raise my son, dear fan,
For you to call him names.
He may not be a superstar
It's just a high school game.

So please don't curse those boys down there,
They do the best they can.
They never tried to lose a game,
They're boys and you're a man.

This game belongs to them, you see,
You're really just a guest,
They do not need a fan like you,
They need the very best.

141

142

143

If you have nothing nice to say,
Please leave the boys alone.
And if you have no manners,
Why don't you stay at home!

So please don't curse those boys down there,
Each one's his parents' son,
And win or lose or tie, you see,
To us, they're number one!

144

Can you imagine finding these verses in a professional football program? *Please don't throw your half-filled bottles at those men down there ...* The Dayton City Schools' program uses an essay from Charles Loftus, the former Director of Sports Information at Yale University, entitled "What Is a Football Player?" Consider this excerpt:

He may not be an All-American, but he is an example of the American way. He is judged, not for his race, not for his religion, not for his social standing and not for his finances, but by the democratic yardstick of how well he blocks, tackles, and sacrifices individual glory for the overall success of the team.

You read and nod your head in agreement. Others do the same. *Well said, Charles. Well said.*

145

141. Libbey Drum Major, Toledo Woodward at Toledo Libbey, 10/27/01

142. Marion Local Band, Mogadore v. Maria Stein Marion Local, Paul Brown Tiger Stadium, 12/1/01

143. Licking Valley Band, Kenton v. Newark Licking Valley, Canton Fawcett Stadium, 12/1/01

144. St. Wendelin Band, Fostoria St. Wendelin v. Oregon Cardinal Stritch, Fostoria Stadium, 9/1/01

145. Bellaire Band, Bellaire v. Richmond Edison, Nelson Field, 9/29/01

You tuck the program under your arm and pick up your order. It's nice milling about in this crowd. You and your hot dog. Gaggles of junior high kids have grouped about the area around the concession stand. Long strands of words rush from their mouths like water from a tipped pitcher. Boys and girls test their mating skills in primitive, awkward ways, hitting, poking, screaming, and wrestling - with everyone watching. You think to yourself, *was flirting ever this easy? At what age did it get so complex? And expensive?* The boys use cologne to cover up their newly realized adult smells while the girls — the same ones you saw walking around the stands throughout the first half — are awash in the saccharine scents of perfume, hairspray, and bubble gum.

146

Ladies and gentlemen! Please welcome the finest band in the land! A woman's voice trills through the PA system, sparkling with enthusiasm and echoing loudly in the homes around the stadium. The pronouncement brings the spectators' attention back to the field. *Tonight they'll take a walk down memory lane performing a medley of your favorite songs from yesterday, today, and tomorrow.* (Favorite songs from tomorrow?) On the far sideline, the band lines up, prepared to cascade across the field, spreading in all directions, following carefully patterned steps, marching in unison with band mates, forming complex shapes and letters (printed and script), moving forwards, backwards, sideways, and diagonally while striking every note and beat on their instruments. No one said athleticism left the field when the half ended.

146. Edgewood Band, Ashtabula Edgewood at Hanoverton United, 8/25/01

147. St. Francis DeSales Band, Painesville Riverside at Columbus St. Francis DeSales, 9/15/01

148. St. Xavier Band, Cincinnati St. Xavier v. Cincinnati Princeton, 11/10/01

149. Indian Valley Band, Gnadenhutten Indian Valley at Uhrichsville Claymont, 10/27/01

150. Shaker Heights Band, Lorain Southview at Shaker Heights, 10/13/01

147

You notice that what the football action may have lacked in pageantry and style is more than compensated for by the band. Where football prides itself on grime and sweat and earthy materials, the band strives for precision, grace, formality, and aesthetics. The band members are cloaked in bulky coats with exaggeratedly square shoulders. Garish plumes sprout from boxy cardboard hats, and oversized brass buttons glitter in the stadium light. Behind the band, the flag corps works together, extending colorful banners into the air like the feathers on a peacock. The flags sashay back and forth in time to the music, twirling in colorful circles and pitching end over end into the air, falling back to earth, still on beat, into waiting hands. Along the near sidelines, majorettes deliver the dance interpretation of the band's musical selections. Dripping in sequins and theatrical make-up, they arch their backs and prance and float and glide through an expansive catalog of steps: fox trots, rumbas, beguines, salsas, bops — all culminating in the standard Rockette-inspired high kicks.

Out in front, standing on three separate five-foot platforms spaced ten yards apart, drum majorettes from Defiance High School direct this scene like traffic cops at the height of rush hour. Dressed in white cowboys hats, white boots, and white satin shorts with royal blue satin jackets, they gesticulate madly, waving their arms left and right in great expressive sweeps. They gyrate and twist and dip with such urgency that you wonder if maybe they're trying to push the music into the stands rather than direct the band. In the center of these three conductors, Danielle Moore watches the horn section step forward for their solos. She and two others were selected for these positions from 22 candidates. Moore is not without her own musical expertise. In the school orchestra and jazz band, she plays clarinet, but during football season she assumes the role of

148

149

150

enthusiastic choirmaster, whipping herself into a melodic frenzy at midfield, sending her passion for performance into the stands and coursing through the band. It's part of the Great Team System at Fred J. Brown Stadium in Defiance. "It's our job to pump up the crowd. If we do that, then hopefully, that'll help the team play better."

In the stands tonight, a semi-secret society has gathered. In fact, they gather at almost every game in almost every stadium throughout the state. They do not stand out. They cheer as loudly as anyone when the team succeeds and demonstrate appropriate disappointment when it loses. They sit among the football fans wearing school colors, following the action with rapt concentration. Yet they are not ashamed of their secret, nor do they fear being discovered among this football crowd. This semi-secret society attends games with slightly different priorities. They are present to support their team, yes, but really they're there *to see the band.*

They hold nothing against the football team; they have a fondness for the game that brings them to the stadium every Friday night. But all those arcane rules and the constant stopping and starting of play, well frankly, it can get a little boring. *Give us the band, they say, give us a show, give us some song and dance, something we can tap our feet to. That's what we want.* As Darrell Lucas, the band director at Bellaire High School, likes to say, "The definition of football is the activity that occurs on either side of the band's halftime show."

Deb Carney from Uhrichsville laughs in agreement when you share that statement with her. Tonight, she beams with pride watching her daughter Lauren play. Her other daughter,

151

152

153

now graduated from Claymont High School, performed in the flag corps, so the draw for Deb and her husband has always been the band. Without reservation, Carney applauds more loudly for the band than the Mustangs. Not out of disrespect for the football team, mind you, but out of deep admiration for the "sport" of marching band. She has watched her daughters devote 10 hours a week to practice during the school year plus one week of band camp and 12-hour practice days during the summer. On top of that, figure in the long bus rides and the hours at the games, sitting in the sun wearing those thick top coats in August and September, and then braving the rain and sleet of October and November. All the while they bear a responsibility for keeping the fans and team motivated with endless renditions of fight songs, light melodies, and cheers. It calls for a commitment that rivals the dedication of any player on the field, although Carney definitely prefers having children in the band rather than on the football team. "I can't imagine what it would be like to see your son get hurt on the field. I don't have to worry about that."

154

Most of today's marching bands fall into one of two categories: show band or competition band. The show band performs a different show each week and opts for more free-wheeling songs that allow a certain level of playfulness and improvisation. The competition band keeps the same routines from week to week and typically prefers the chestnuts of the band world, songs from well-known movies and musicals that lend themselves to less spontaneity, but require a higher level of musicianship and choreographic precision.

155

156

151. Newcomerstown Band, Newcomerstown v. Bowerston Conotton Valley, 10/20/01

152 Kenton Band, Kenton v. Newark Licking Valley, Canton Fawcett Stadium, 12/1/01

153. Edison Band, Bellaire v. Richmond Edison, Nelson Field, 9/29/01

154. The Piqua "Indian," 9/21/01

155. Lake Catholic Band, Mentor Lake Catholic v. Columbus St. Francis DeSales, Paul Brown Tiger Stadium, 11/30/01

156. Troy Band, Piqua at Troy, 9/21/01

Tonight, band directors David Schwartz and Sal Lovano have blurred these lines. As Steve Curtis and Lou Mains were elected to prepare tonight's field, so Schwartz and Lovano have been called upon to direct the band. Tonight, the band performs a medley of Oscar-winning soundtracks and rock tunes from the 1970s. It's a fun mix, unpredictable, and the shifting tempos keep the audience on guard and attentive. Schwartz, from Painesville Riverside, stands behind the drum majorettes and watches the band move through its routine. He has selected the movie songs, a seamless medley that runs through passages from *Raiders of the Lost Ark, Star Wars, Bridge Over the River Kwai, and Patton.* At Riverside, Schwartz personally arranges all the music the band will play throughout the year. He understands that marching band, like football, has its own culture, its own ecology that plays a crucial role in making the band play better and, more importantly, helping teach kids how to socialize and get along with others. During the 2001 season, Schwartz and his assistants will leave extra early for an away game. On the way, the Riverside band will stop at a park and hold their own Band Olympics. It's one small way that the directors can instill a sense of team among a group of 175 students.

> " I JUST HAVE TO BEAT THE DRUMS. SHAKE THE STICK, AND RUN AROUND. I CAN HANDLE THAT MUCH. IF IT GETS INTO DANCES, I CAN'T DO IT."
>
> Matthew Reichman,
> Mascot, Piqua H.S.

When the band finishes its run from Harrison Ford to George C. Scott, Lovano from Richmond Edison High School replaces Schwartz behind the band majorettes and quietly rocks out as the band shifts into a new gear, looser and with added verve. The first tune is vaguely familiar, but you can't quite place it. *This is definitely not John Phillip Sousa. Could it be? Naw. Well, maybe ... yeah, it is. Yes, they're playing Funkadelic!* Lovano notes your odd grin of recognition and lets out a huge laugh.

157

157. McComb v. Columbus Grove, 11/17/01

158. Ohio Hill Country Coal Festival Queens, Wellston, 9/7/01

159. Homecoming King & Queen, Dayton Meadowdale, 10/6/01

160. Homecoming Attendants, Baltimore Liberty Union, 9/28/01

161. Homecoming King & Queen, Niles McKinley., 10/11/01

Wearing longish black hair and slick sunglasses, he carries on the tradition of Ohio University's Marching 110, a band famous for its irreverent and exceptional style of play. He takes pleasure in finding songs that one might think couldn't possibly be translated for a marching band. In his 19 years as a director, Lovano has arranged music from Styx; Van Halen; and Emerson, Lake & Palmer; and the Edison band reflects this unconventional repertoire. Some wear French berets, others wear Lovano-like sunglasses, and all of them engage in unusual field antics, doing push-ups, sit spins, and free-lance jigs. The band members, he tells you, were initially reluctant to dance and hop around the field, but when they saw how much the crowd enjoyed the show, they let it all hang out.

158

As the horns blare and the woodwinds croon and the bass drums send sonorous thumps hurtling into outer space, you think about the way music makes this scene whole. The way *Hark! The Herald Angel Sings* creates a sense of warmth and belonging around a decorated Christmas tree, so we form powerful associations between a school's fight song and a football stadium. It gives the environment a certain richness, makes the field greener, the air fresher, and the game more exciting. You know, it can be a little unsettling to watch a live game without hearing the band, like watching a sit-com without the laugh track. You're not completely sure what to cheer, and when you do cheer, you don't have the band to act as the natural extension of your excitement and take your celebration to a level that your lungs cannot reach. We all need to hear the band.

159

160

161

Inside the locker room, the teams are making final adjustments for the second half. The players have scattered about the room by position, and now they watch intently as the coaches hastily scribble plays and formations on wipe-it boards. Trainers tip-toe through the crowded space, circulating water bottles and ministering to injured players and damaged equipment. The halftime break has served its purpose. When the team entered, sweat dripped from their chins, feet dragged, and the players sat down hard. As the coaches wind up their halftime speeches, the bright faces have returned, and the cleats are tapping again. Let the second half begin.

162

163

164

162. Jefferson Band, Delphos Jefferson v. Ada,
     Delphos Stadium Park, 9/22/01

163. Libbey Band, Toledo Woodward at Toledo Libbey, 10/27/01

164. East Liverpool Band, East Liverpool at Steubenville,10/19/01

165. Poland Seminary Band, New Middletown Springfield at
     Poland Seminary, 8/24/01

167

166. Toledo St. Francis DeSales v.
Columbus Bishop Watterson,
Paul Brown Tiger Stadium, 11/30/01

167. Piqua at Troy, 9/21/01

168. Kenton v. Newark Licking Valley,
Canton Fawcett Stadium, 12/1/01

169. Mogadore v. Maria Stein Marion Local,
Paul Brown Tiger Stadium, 12/1/01

ACROSS MANY FIELDS

THIRDQUARTER

ALTHOUGH you came to this game with a few doubts, you have to admit it's been entertaining so far. Following all the team changes hasn't been easy, but it has been entertaining. You've met some interesting people, too. And there are definitely enough field fireworks to keep your focus on the game. That happens sometimes — you lose interest in the game. Not so much that you'd consider going home or doing something else, but there are momentary zone-outs where you get lost in your own thoughts or have your attention drawn from the field. It's like being too snug in the easy chair at home: You want to watch the show on television, but darn it, *that chair*. It's so soft and comfortable, the cushions seem to wrap around you and inject sleeping potion into your unsuspecting veins. Fortunately, as with most television shows these days, you can easily regain your spot in a football game. Just take a look at the field and the scoreboard, and give a quick listen to the crowd. You'll be up to speed in no time. When you think about it, your tendency to miss a play here and there says less about your interest in the game and more about your level of security and ease. Now you understand those Saturday and Sunday afternoons when your father appeared to be slumbering away in front of a televised game, how he startled awake the minute you touched the dial and blurted out, in a froggy voice, *Hey, I'm watching that*. As near and dear as we hold football to our hearts, it's sometimes just the preferred white noise of Ohioans.

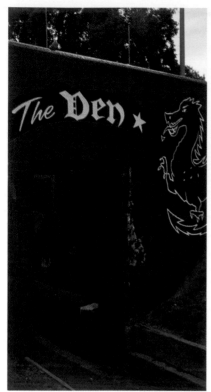

170

171

For the second half you decide to sit on the other side of the field. Actually, you have no choice. Your excursion to the press box during the first half cost you a seat. As you stood with the videographers, the amoebic crowd slithered sideways and gobbled your seat up whole. Fortunately, you see a few clear benches in the top row of the opposite stands. With luck, maybe you'll be able to wiggle your way into an open space, a tiny patch of aluminum with just enough room so that your knees aren't implanted in the meaty portion of someone's back, with just enough room to let you rise upright when a big play calls you from your seat.

You head toward one end of the field, walking along the chain link fence that circles the playing field and the synthetic running track. Men lean languorously against the fence, transferring as much body weight as possible from their feet to the metal posts. When you arrived this evening, nearly all of them wore baseball hats and t-shirts, but now some of them have exchanged those items for light stocking caps, flannel-lined coats, and rain gear. Rain gear? Yes, rain gear. Far above the field, miles beyond the illumination, dense clouds moved stealthily into position. While the games raged on, isolated in themselves like fake winter scenes suspended in snow globes, you ignored the portentous breezes that whooshed across the field, foretelling frigid and steady rain. Your immediate reaction is regret and disappointment. Adverse weather is football's Great Equalizer. It can make good teams bad and bad teams as good as better teams. It softens the field as it softens the spirits of the spectators, taking their night of casual observation and turning it into an endurance contest.

172

170. Bo Rein Stadium, Niles McKinley, 10/11/01

171. Harding Stadium, Steubenville, 10/19/01

172. Harding Stadium, Steubenville, 10/19/01

173. McComb v. Columbus Grove, Lima Stadium, 11/17/01

173

But isn't the weather just one more thing you should cherish about football? Doesn't bad weather bestow a certain respect on football fans, make them even more special for their willingness to brave inclement conditions?   Yes, you think it does. Remember what Brad Bunting, an assistant coach for Baltimore Liberty Union, said: "With football, you can play it no matter what. If it's raining, you can play. If it's cold, you can play. If it's snowing, you can play. You can't do that with other sports." True enough, but all the same you'd rather be dry and unencumbered by restrictive clothing. A single drop of rain plinks on the back of your hand. It's cold, cold water. The drop clings to your skin and sends a chill through your body. Another sign of winter marching closer.

You reach the goal posts and stop for a minute to look at the whole stadium from a new perspective. The bleachers climb at an angle, enclosing a small emerald valley. Those first few drops of rain have triggered the release of fluorescent rain ponchos in the stands; they sprout bright orange, bright yellow, and bright green. A few intrepid souls have put up umbrellas, but you suspect they will be quickly asked to put those away. *Down in front! Can't see! Can't see! Would you mind lowering your umbrella? Thank you.* The stadium lights pad the field in a heavenly glow. The players casually stretch in the final seconds of halftime, bathing in surreal daylight, trying to make out familiar faces among the shadowy figures in the bleachers.

You admire high school stadiums, these miniature cathedrals of play. They carry as much structural significance as a city hall or court house, unmistakable in purpose.

174. Piqua at Troy, 9/21/01

175. Columbus World Harvest Academy v.
Yellow Springs, Pickerington Stadium,
9/15/01

176. Cincinnati St. Xavier v. Cleveland St.
Ignatius, Canton Fawcett Stadium, 12/1/01

174

You think of Piqua. The Indians' home field moved from the industrial section of down-town out to Alexander Park, a spacious pitch behind the school, bordered on three sides by corn fields. Its spotless white concrete and unblemished paint remind you of an amusement park at the start of the summer. Clearly, Piqua's stadium must surpass those of many small colleges.

Even though every field must extend exactly 120 yards, each stadium still displays a fingerprint-like uniqueness. In Chesapeake, U.S. Route 52 traces along the north side of the stadium, which is situated below the road. Tired drivers (or those unable to find suitable radio entertainment) can pull off to the berm, perch on a guardrail, and watch the Panthers do battle below. In Lima, men carry folding chairs to Lima Senior Stadium and line up along the fence outside the North end zone. It's a partially obstructed and distant view, but the admission is free, and if the Spartans aren't using the field that night, they're not much interested in paying for a better seat anyhow. When taking the field in Plymouth, the players follow a trail leading from the school's parking lot to Mary Fate city park. There, among the swing sets, slides, and merry-go-rounds, the Big Red performs for the town faithful. Sandusky High School and St. Mary's Central Catholic share a humongous stadium with tall, forbidding cement walls that look like they were modeled after a penitentiary. Like many other high school stadiums throughout Ohio, Sandusky's Stroebel Field was built as part of the Works Progress Administration during the Depression. When the Blue Streaks and Panthers host games today, the events pay continuing homage to the men who worked so hard when work was so scarce.

175

When you think of all the things the government might have assigned for construction in the early 1930s, why high school stadiums? Yes, extra-curriculars have long been an integral part of American schooling, but might there have been something else? During the Depression, the popularity of movies skyrocketed. People filed into theaters in unprecedented numbers. Inside, in the darkened hush, they could leave their unfortunate conditions for a few hours. In similar fashion, spectator sports could provide a temporary reprieve from the troubling circumstances of the outside world.

176

Although our economic conditions are improved today, sports still offer that same release from the mundane. Modern athletes struggle for victory with balletic leaps, thunderous collisions, and free-flowing force. It represents a style of living that occupies a shrinking space in modern civilization. In the workplace, we toil in environments where strong feelings are discouraged and goals are always one step ahead. In the stadium, the parameters are clearly defined (10 yards for a first down, three points for a field goal), and unfettered emotion is the norm. In the stadium, we can be like that person we can't be in the workplace. We can cheer and shout and groan at any volume we like. We can be and see so many things that our regular lives do not offer. It's escape. And who knows where it can lead?

In Van Wert, the Cougars closed out the 2000 regular season by losing three of their last five games, including a dismal 41-7 thrashing in the finale, and yet they still managed to

177

limp into the playoffs with a 6-4 record. Needless to say, expectations were not overly high. In the first two rounds, they posted decisive wins over Sunbury Big Walnut and Bellevue, and the townsfolk said, *Well, whaddya know? Maybe we're not so bad!* Round three pitted Van Wert against perennial state power Columbus Bishop Watterson, but the Cougars were a changed team by then. Backed by their boisterous, but well-rehearsed student section, "The Cat Pack," Van Wert battled to a 13-7 victory. Surely, people thought, this win would mark the end of the road as the state semifinal game brought a match-up against a Portsmouth team that averaged roughly 40 points a game during the regular season while posting five shutouts. But something had happened during these first three rounds. Van Wert's team discovered they could play good football, and the town rallied behind their sudden outbreak of inspiration and success. Together, the Cougars and the people of Van Wert started dreaming about the possibilities and escaping the mental limitations that had plagued the team during the regular season.

On a late November night in Grove City Stadium, the Cougars posted a fourth quarter touchdown for a dramatic 28-21 win over the previously unbeaten Trojans. Just like that, this near-.500 team had found itself in the state finals where they would take on the Crusaders from Canton Central Catholic. On the day of that game, most of the town packed up and headed east on U.S. Route 30 toward Fawcett Stadium in Canton. Van Wert had been to the playoffs in 1985 and 1986, but those were quick, unremarkable first round exits, footnotes consigned to dusty team pictures hanging in the

178

school lobby. The state finals! — now this was rarefied air the town was breathing, and it rushed through the people like nitrous oxide, making them giddy with anticipation and conjecture. *Do you think we can win? What if we won? What would that be like? Wouldn't that be great?* And for a while, everyone forgot that Van Wert was a small farming town near the Indiana border saddled with many typical anxieties — school, employment, finances, time, health, weather, and politics. They left it all behind that day to watch their *(their)* young men do battle in the name of Van Wert.

Let's not mince words. It *does* matter that Van Wert lost that day. And it is also significant that they lost after two overtimes. By one point. It would not help to think that these facts made the loss less difficult to accept. Tears were shed that December afternoon, and hearts were harshly rent. The loss brought the people of Van Wert crashing back to earth, some even a bit regretful for the rapid rise if only because it made the descent so much more uncontrollable. One hundred and ninety-three teams in Ohio have never made the playoffs, and far fewer have ever whiffed the pleasing air of a state final game. As the Van Wert players and fans walked away that evening with the scoreboard showing 27-26 in favor of the Crusaders, they would carry home the memories of this journey and the muscle-tense anguish of an improbable playoff run and double-overtime loss. Those feelings would be *theirs forever*, banked in the town's collective memory. That's why it matters.

The only thing that matters to you right now is finding a way to escape the steady downpour. The teams have taken the field for the second half kickoff just as you find a seat along the back row of the stands. A woman next to you loans you a seat cushion to place

179. Vanlue Wildcats, Vanlue, 8/31/01

180. Bedford St. Peter Chanel v. Marion Pleasant, Canton Fawcett Stadium, 11/30/01

181. McComb v. Columbus Grove, Lima Stadium, 11/17/01

179

over your head. On the sidelines, the players' helmets glisten with beads of water, and some have pulled on vinyl-coated parkas. All around you heads are covered, some with rain hoods, others with folded-up trash bags or rain-drenched programs.

Across the field, near the entrance gates, you can see a few people heading for the parking lot with quickening strides. You have no idea who those people are, nor what team they root for, but you know they're not parents. Parents don't go home when the weather turns bad. Parents stick it out. Parents clean uniforms and keep dinner warm in the oven after a late practice. Parents pick you up and drop you off at countless practices. Parents applaud when injured players walk off the field, regardless of which uniform they wear. Parents cheer with an intensity that comes from an area between the heart and stomach, that tender space in the center of their chests where all the years of love and hope they carry for their children reside. You think a little rain is going to chase away some parents?

In front of you, Greg Siefring chuckles to himself and exclaims, "Look at those people leaving." Siefring, a resident of Coldwater and father of a former cheerleader, would never leave a game early. It wouldn't be a good example for the kids, and examples are what make Coldwater teams special. How else can you explain a Division 4 state-runner up team that loses 14 starters and makes the state semifinals the next year? That kind of success would require immense dedication and teamwork, the kind that can only be learned from parents. In Coldwater's case that means the hard-working descendents of Dutch and German immigrants who carved out a home in the plains of west central Ohio. The Coldwater Cavaliers have examples to follow.

Consider Coldwater head coach John Reed. You can safely assume a coach with six playoff appearances in seven years must be a good motivator, strategist, and teacher. But when you ask Siefring what makes Reed a good coach, he says without hesitation, "John Reed is a true gentleman." *What!? What about Leo Durocher and nice guys finishing last and no one remembering who finished second? Gentleman? Aw, come on!* You're tempted to say these things to Siefring, but then he talks about Coldwater's 2000 state final loss to Youngstown Ursuline, an awesomely talented team with a gargantuan offensive line, an all-state quarterback, and two tailbacks that gained over 1,000 yards each during the regular season. From the outset, it was clear Ursuline was the more gifted squad, but the Cavs hung tough behind 422 passing yards from quarterback Kyle Hoyng. Ursuline's Fighting Irish would eventually prevail, 49-37. When Siefring recalls this game, he chokes up describing its aftermath. He doesn't gnash his teeth at the thought of what might have been. Instead he melts, remembering the display of emotion, children and adults alike sharing a post-game moment of comfort, hugs and heads and arms all grouped together, collectively dressing the wound of goal desired and goal denied. You miss those moments if you leave the game early. Parents don't miss those moments.

A murmur riffs through the crowd. Several people point down to the field. You try to see what exactly they're pointing at. There are two new teams on the field. It appears they're pointing at the tight end for the team with the red jerseys. You don't recognize him. The woman next to you says, *That's Kelly Cole from Vanlue.* Hmm. Cole from Vanlue. It doesn't ring a bell. *Kelly? Oh.* Cole isn't one of those boy Kellys. She's a young woman, Kelly. Interesting. She is indeed a special player, worthy of some attention

182

183

tonight, but not because she defies the unspoken gender rules of the sport. Her gender has never been the issue, most certainly when playing for Vanlue head coach Tony Fenstermaker. From day one, he told Cole and her teammates that there would be no exemptions or lowered expectations for her performance. Of course, some arrangements are required. Cole dresses in a separate locker room for practice, and when the Wildcats hit the road, she must ride the bus already dressed in uniform since there will only be one locker room for the team in their opponent's stadium.

What makes Kelly Cole special is why she plays. In the no-stoplight town of Vanlue, a farming community southeast of Findlay that has not won a Blanchard Valley Conference football game in almost ten years, players are hard to come by. Vanlue sits near the bottom in terms of eligible male population for high school athletics. Not all of these young men can be persuaded to play football; some play in the band. A typical Vanlue team fields between 15 and 20 players, not even enough for a live scrimmage, only hours and hours of drill. With just a couple sprained ankles and a small flu bug, the Wildcats could be faced with a forfeit.

Senior Kevin Cole, Kelly's older brother, plays tailback for Vanlue. His sister wanted to do what she could to insure that Kevin would be able to play all ten games, so she came out for the team. The contact would be a marked change from Kelly's other sport, volleyball, but she welcomed the chance to scrum it up with her brother and his friends, and she has the bruised arms to prove it. Kevin, meanwhile, heard concerns from his teammates and some of his conference opponents. *I just don't feel right about hitting*

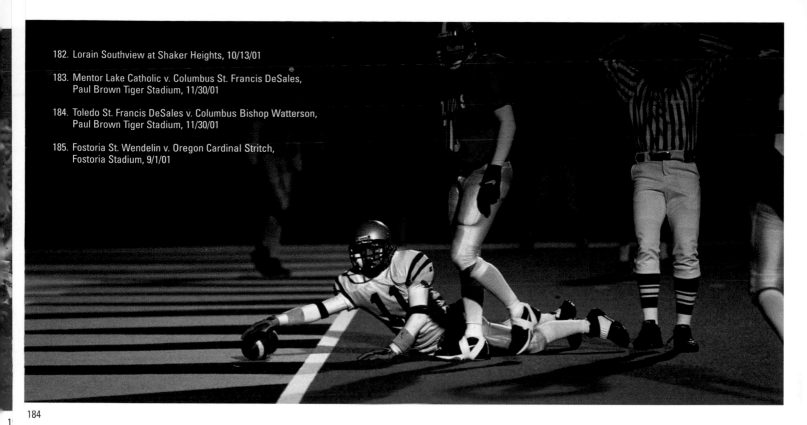

182. Lorain Southview at Shaker Heights, 10/13/01

183. Mentor Lake Catholic v. Columbus St. Francis DeSales,
      Paul Brown Tiger Stadium, 11/30/01

184. Toledo St. Francis DeSales v. Columbus Bishop Watterson,
      Paul Brown Tiger Stadium, 11/30/01

185. Fostoria St. Wendelin v. Oregon Cardinal Stritch,
      Fostoria Stadium, 9/1/01

184

1

your sister, man. I don't want to hurt her. Kevin knew better. He knew she could take the contact — and deal some out, too. He told everyone who asked, "Hey, do anything you want, just don't play dirty." Fair enough. When Fenstermaker passed out team jerseys at the start of the year, Kelly took 88, the same number her father wore for Vanlue many years ago. She is a special player, indeed.

The rain's intensity has picked up, still steady, but heavier now, a wide open tap from the sky. The gridiron has been transformed into a sponge at this point, holding water, getting softer and softer by the second. With each new play, the field sheds more clumps of turf, cut loose by hundreds of forceful cleated steps. Large patches of thick mud pock the once unspoiled stretches of green. Widening plots of mud wait for a loose foot or an unsteady heel, and threaten to turn an ordinary play into a wild, drop-your-coffee-in-your-lap game breaker.

185

As the wind starts to blow the rain sideways from goal post to goal post, Plymouth and Ashland Mapleton come into view on the field. These Firelands conference opponents have struggled during the 2001 campaign, and they will not advance beyond the game you're watching, because this action is taken from week 10 of the regular season. Both teams are Division 6 schools, both teams feature young players in the lineup, and both teams have come to the field tonight for a last bit of competition before they hand in their equipment. More importantly, this game would be for the seniors, most

The rain has ceased, for the time being, as a second-round playoff game emerges through the portal. The royal blue of Cincinnati St. Xavier and regal red of Cincinnati Princeton move into view. You might call this pairing the Battle of Old and New. Old is Princeton, a perennial powerhouse from the 1970s through the early 90s, who, under legendary coach Pat Mancuso, appeared in six state title games, taking home first prize in three of those. Since Mancuso's departure, however, Princeton has struggled to find its old form. New is St. Xavier — although the school, established in 1840, can hardly be considered as such. In the 1990s, the Bombers earned two state final berths. The 2001 season would find St. Xavier and veteran coach Steve Rasso in a third state championship game.

Princeton's third-year head coach, Scott Miltenberger, has resurrected some of the old Viking glory this season. Through the formidable Greater Miami Conference, he has led Princeton to a playoff appearance, their first in eight years. After a rather easy first-round win over Cincinnati Anderson, the Vikings ran up against St. Xavier, a team that finished the regular season ranked number one in the state, posting impressive wins against Cincinnati Elder, Hamilton, and Cleveland St. Ignatius. Coming into the Princeton match-up, the Bombers had averaged a cool 30 points per game while posting three shut-outs. St. Xavier's offense moved largely on the accurate passing arm of senior quarterback Marty Mooney, who stood continually poised and secure behind a huge offensive line, featuring all-state lineman Kyle Ralph. In fact, the entire Bombers' offensive line looks like a fleet of semis with helmets. Princeton's order on the game would be a tall and challenging one.

The scene you're watching, however, has St. Xavier on defense. Their primary objective for this game is containing Princeton's dual offensive threats: an elusive and resourceful

194

192. Avon Lake at Amherst Steele, 10/12/01

193. Bellaire v. Richmond Edison,
Nelson Field, 9/29/01

194. Kenton v. Newark Licking Valley,
Canton Fawcett Stadium, 12/1/01

195. Lakewood St. Edward v. Cleveland
St. Ignatius, Lakewood Stadium, 10/13/01

quarterback named Mike Daniels, and his favorite receiver, the greyhound-quick Darren Barnett. Trailing 6-0, Daniels takes a shotgun snap from center. Within seconds, St. Xavier linemen break through, forcing Daniels to roll out to his right. Keeping the ball positioned in his passing hand, the quarterback looks vainly for an open receiver. Standing only 5'8," he quickly disappears from view beneath the rush of Bombers. At the last moment, before the human avalanche swarms over him, Daniels spins out, á la Fran Tarkenton, and reverses field to his left. Daniels wants to throw; his steps become choppy as he slows to plant himself. Still, no receiver appears, and the Bombers quickly close the gap. Daniels is standing almost still now, and you think you can see drool hanging off the facemasks of the St. Xavier linemen. A lineman reaches an arm toward the quarterback as he starts to throw. The collision interrupts the flight of the ball. It squirts clumsily into the air, looping high, allowing several defenders time to change direction. As the ball topples end over end in the air, the crowd

195

gasps, and gasps again as a Princeton player and St. Xavier player hurl themselves forward. They crash mightily into each other, but to no avail. The ball thuds softly on the turf, wobbles a moment, and then lies still. The crowd resumes normal breathing.

The referee calls timeout, examines the ball and sends it to the side judge with a looping underhanded throw that is the trademark of football officials. One of the laces has come loose, and this ball will need to be replaced. The side judge looks for the ball boys, but the young men on the sidelines stand there empty handed, clueless and innocent,

196. Mogadore v. Maria Stein Marion Local,
Paul Brown Tiger Stadium, 12/1/01

197. Mansfield Ontario v. Castalia Margaretta,
W.W. Skiles Field, Shelby, 11/10/01

196

grinning back at the official. With a serious look, the side judge sends them in a frantic dash to find another ball.

It's just one more of the glamorless duties that are the domain of the football official. Officials are the bartenders of the football cosmos. They hear all the gripes and clean up all the spills. Their faces evince a world-weary resignation that says: *I've seen it all before. You cannot shock me.* Sure, they call the shots on the field, but their authoritative respon-

> "THE KIDS RUN OVER AND GIVE ME A HIGH-FIVE AND I'M 50 YEARS OLD. THAT'S PRETTY NICE."
>
> Gary Arnett, Statistician, Waverly H.S.

sibilities are offset by the mundane tasks of checking equipment and staying out of the way. Think about it. When do you see a football official on the TV news? When they hawkeye movement in the offensive line prior to the snap? Not usually. Officials make the highlight reel when they blow a call, or more often, when they get bowled over by a pile of players, looking like rodeo clowns caught under the charging feet of Fernando the Dyspeptic Bull.

Staying out of the way, however, is actually the point. Most officials, like 28-year veteran Jim Lanese, a former Cleveland public school teacher, will tell you that when a crew is on top of their game, they should be "invisible" on the field. Like party hosts, they keep everything civil, yet entertaining. Years ago, the Cleveland *Plain Dealer* newspaper featured a front page picture of a high school receiver making a crucial touchdown catch late in the game. There's another figure in the picture, but it's blurred from view and difficult to make out except that you can tell it's not a player. It's Lanese — on top of the play and making the right call. He said he cut out that picture and had it enlarged to remind himself of his role: running a fair

game and staying away from the forefront. It's reassuring, then, to remember these officials. In today's media-crazed culture, with so many people mugging for cameras and willing to debase themselves for a little air time, we have a set of adults who make it their optimal goal to get on a public stage and become "invisible" for the sake of fair play.

A new ball has been located. Brad Yoder had been standing around filming the game with his camcorder, but when he saw the officials looking for a ball, he immediately hit the "pause" button and joined in the hunt. It's exactly the reaction you'd expect from a booster. Yoder has served six years as booster club president for Malvern High School. During the year, he travels to all the Hornet games to film the action. After the season, those tapes are edited for highlights, set to a contemporary soundtrack of inspirational rock songs, and given to the outgoing senior players as a gift. How times have changed since the original booster clubs of Massillon, when Paul Brown asked boosters to contribute enough money to buy one meal a day for every player!

The dedication has grown with the sport. As players now train for football year round, so do boosters pound the pavement, looking for ways to support the athletic programs. Portsmouth's Skip Kyle can give you a tour of the Trojans' spiffy team bus, used not only by the football team, he tells you, but all Portsmouth athletic teams as well as Portsmouth Notre Dame High School. Kyle refers to himself as the "Chief Scrounger" for Portsmouth, and it's a title he speaks with pride, a pride borne from an early awareness of a town's mutually reinforcing relationship with its athletic teams.

198

When Kyle was 13 years old, his grandmother was preparing to take him and his sister to the Portsmouth/Ironton game, the most anticipated game of the year between the Ohio River rivals. Just before leaving, Kyle's grandmother asked him to fetch a roll of quarters from her dresser and a tube sock from his own. She dropped the quarters into the sock and tied off the open end with a firm knot. Kyle timidly asked what she was doing. The old woman replied imperiously, "you don't think I'm going to an Ironton game without something to defend myself? Those people are crazy." Sometimes boosterism works in mysterious ways.

Mansfield Ontario's Warriors and Castalia Margaretta's Polar Bears have come onto the field. On defense, the Polar Bears stand imposingly larger than the quicker, more athletic Warriors. In the middle of the Polar Bears' defense looms fullback and line-backer, John Sessler, whose helmet looks like it was dragged 100 miles behind a pick-up truck on a gravel road. So far tonight, the Warriors have been unable to slow down the 245-pound senior who has scored two touchdowns, and picked up several key first downs. Ontario, meanwhile, is scrambling to keep their playoff run alive. Coming off an undefeated regular season, the Warriors won their first-round game, routing the Vikings of Marion River Valley, 42-0.

The scene playing out for you is from late in the fourth quarter with Margaretta leading 13-0. A sense of urgency pervades the Ontario sidelines. The Warriors know they must score quickly if they want to get back into this game. Quarterback Travis Weirich sets himself under center and starts the snap count. Fans on both sides of the field sit motion-less, their muscles tense with anticipation. Weirich takes the ball, drops two steps and

199

198. Dayton Meadowdale v. Portsmouth,
Dayton Welcome Stadium, 10/6/01

199. Marion Pleasant v. Liberty Center,
Findlay Donnell Stadium, 11/16/01

200. Drum Majorette, Defiance Band,
Fred J. Brown Stadium, 8/31/01

fires a slant pass to number 32, Ian Craze. Craze, a junior split end, has averaged 20-plus yards a catch this season, but has yet to break a long-gainer tonight. He bolts straight ahead, sniffing out open lanes like a mouse in a laboratory maze. *Down this road. Nope. Dead end. This way. Wrong again. How about this way?* And so it goes, Craze scurrying back and forth, weaving in and out of green and white Polar Bear uniforms at implausibly sharp angles. He springs free of traffic near the Margaretta 20-yard line and darts into the end zone, leaving a wake of fallen defenders like twisted human wreckage. The Ontario sideline erupts in celebration, cheered momentarily by the glimmer of hope returned to their playoff aspirations. Alas, they fall short in this contest. Sessler, center Kevin Van Ness, and the rest of the Polar Bear offense run out the clock on the next possession, piling up spirit-killing first downs, until the clock reads 0:00.

200

The number of teams you have a chance of watching this evening has shrunk considerably. Earlier in the game, during the first and second quarters, it was a real grab bag, impossible to predict what the portal would emit for your viewing pleasure. Seven hundred and eight teams started the 2001 season, but now, after round two of the playoffs, only 48 remain, less than seven percent. The long and winding road grows narrower. Now you see more players in the stands. They wear varsity jackets in school colors, having come to cheer for (or against) the teams who won their conference or perhaps ended their own playoff run. They've come out tonight for another dose of Friday night, holding onto the autumn air and one last breath of gridiron escape, until winter will finally force them to put the season away.

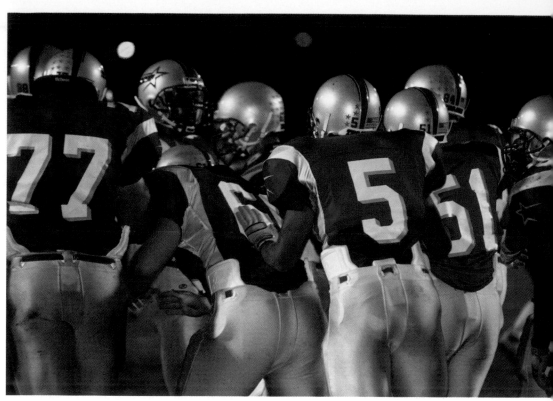

201

201. Piqua at Troy, 9/21/01

202. Lorain Southview at Shaker Heights, 10/13/01

203. Windham at Southington Chalker, 8/25/01

As you watch these young men swirl through the crowd, unusual combinations abound. We've got Jeeps (South Webster), Electrics (Philo), Whippets (Shelby), Tarblooders (Cleveland Glenville), Railroaders (Collinwood), Truckers (Norwalk), Yeomen (Oberlin), Little Giants (Fremont Ross), Aces (Amanda-Clearcreek), Orientals (Akron East), Punchers (Columbus Mifflin), Smithies (Smithville), Cruisers (Groveport-Madison), Locomotives (Montpelier) and another hundred Bulldogs, Eagles, Tigers, Wildcats, and Panthers. As the third quarter ends, the cloud cover takes a cue and moves on. Just like that. You wish that meant a comfortable fourth quarter, but colder air sweeps across the field now, crystallizing the traces of water left by the storm. On the sidelines, the cheerleaders dig into their duffel bags for long pants and knit hats, while the players pace the sidelines with their hands overhead, extending four fingers into the air. Sit tight. The do-or-die contests will begin shortly.

203

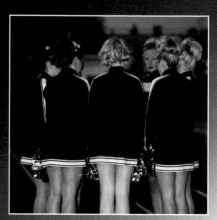

204

204. Sandusky St. Mary's Central
Catholic v. Sandusky Perkins,
Sandusky Stadium, 10/20/01

205. Marion Pleasant v. Liberty Center,
Findlay Donnell Stadium, 11/16/01

206. McComb v. Columbus Grove,
Lima Stadium, 11/17/01

207. Mentor Lake Catholic v. Columbus
St. Francis DeSales, Paul Brown
Tiger Stadium, 11/30/01

AS THE REMAINING TEAMS change directions between quarters, the band fires up. It's a familiar song, and a catchy tune at that. You find yourself humming along. *Hail to the victors valiant, Hail to the conqu'ring heroes. Hail! Hail! To… Wait a second! The Michigan Fight Song! Infidels! Infidels in our stadium!* Well, not quite. All sorts of musical transgressions have occurred tonight. This is just the first one you've noticed. Earlier they played "On Wisconsin," the Notre Dame fight song, the "Trojan March," and of course, "Across the Field." Most high school bands, it seems, co-opt collegiate fight songs, compose their own lyrics, and make the song their own. Who knows why it happened this way. For most schools, it was probably the easiest thing to do short of hiring a composer or compelling the school's music teacher to create a memorable tune. From another perspective, using collegiate fight songs also testifies to the importance and value of tradition at these games. They help pass on a segment of life that can be enjoyed and remembered by multiple generations and provide connections across the ages. Your grandparents heard "Across the Field" the same way you have. These songs make a high school football game sound like a high school football game. It's what we've come to know as football's musical score: the piping horns, the twinkling bells, the thunderous drums, and *rah-rah-rah,* and *sis-boom-bah!*

206

Tradition. It starts with names. Paul Brown. Woody Hayes. Archie Griffin. Chris Spielman. Eddie George. Mention a couple of these names to the person sitting next to you. You'll get a recognition rate on par with some of our nation's presidents. True, these

207

FOURTHQUARTER

are just names, names of actual people who led and lead actual lives doing actual things. But they've also made that tricky ascent into lore, that realm of dual understanding, at once a personal signifier and trigger of runaway memory and meaning. You think for a minute … *Archie Griffin. Graduate of Eastmoor High School in Columbus. Two-time Heisman award winner. The only two-time winner. Number 45 for the Buckeyes. Rambling down the field in Ohio Stadium, "the Horseshoe." Huge games, packed houses, countless tailgates. Scarlet and gray for miles around. Interstate 270 choked with cars. Saturday afternoons on the couch with your dad, with your brother, with your mother, rooting for the Buckeyes. A family room table filled with snacks. Feeling close to your family, comfortable and happy. Sharing the thrill of a Buckeye game; more often than not, a Buckeye victory. Talking about that game over dinner. Talking some more the next day as you read statistics aloud from the morning paper. Going outside and seeing your neighbor, talking about the Bucks game some more. Did you see Archie? Was he amazing or what? Your neighbor laughs and smiles and gives his own version of the game. You get together with your friends for a game of football in the field behind the elementary school. Today, you are Archie Griffin. Today, you can be as good as Archie Griffin. Number 45 for the Buckeyes. I am Archie Griffin.*

Thanks, Archie.

It has been said that The Beatles were great because they were the best at what everyone wanted to be. For Ohio football fans, men like Griffin — and Brown, Hayes, Spielman, George — represent the same ideal. To root for them is to connect with something larger than yourself. To take up their pursuits is to empathize with their journeys. To watch

208

208. Mentor Lake Catholic v. Columbus St. Francis DeSales, Paul Brown Tiger Stadium, 11/30/01

209. Steubenville v. East Liverpool, Harding Stadium, 10/19/01

them succeed is to feel part of yourself grow, expand, and embrace challenge. To watch them fail can be devastating.

Thoughts like these warm you, but all the same you wish you had gloves. You wish you had remembered to bring a hat. You wish you had a thick pair of Carhartt coveralls. You wish that wasn't snow falling on the head of the person in front of you. But it is, and there's nothing you can do about it. What do you expect? Here it is, the fourth quarter, late in the year, in Ohio, a four-season state. On the field, the snow and plummeting temperatures are joining forces to make this game a true test of resolve. Players stamp their feet to keep the blood flowing. The referees and coaches blow into their cupped hands for warmth. That plush green shag from the start of the game has been transformed into a frosty field with jagged edges of icy turf pointing skyward, waiting for human soft spots.

This night has been rife with surprises. Not of the monumental sort, and nothing that could shake your faith or send you dashing to the bank to close all your accounts. Just small incongruencies that cause a double-take — or two, or ten. Earlier tonight, just before the start of the second half, you watched Ryan Keenan from Lakewood St. Edward and John Kerr from Cleveland St. Ignatius huddle close together on the sidelines, talking with easy, comfortable smiles. You don't know if these two young men are friends off the field, but you certainly know that they're not supposed to be friendly *on* the field.

"COACHING IS WHO I AM. IT'S BECOME MY IDENTITY. I DON'T THINK I HAVE ONE IF I DON'T SERVE IN THIS CAPACITY.... AND I'M VERY COMFORTABLE SAYING THAT. I'M PROUD TO SAY I'M A FOOTBALL COACH."

Thom McDaniels, Head Coach,
Warren Harding H.S.

On the west side of Cleveland, many eighth-grade boys in Catholic grade schools are faced with a serious choice. To be a St. Edward Eagle or a St. Ignatius Wildcat: That is the question. Whether 'tis nobler to don the green and gold on Detroit Avenue, or make a slightly longer commute to West 30th and honor the navy blue paw. After grade school, young men who once sat next to each other in class and whose families broke donuts together in the gym after Sunday Mass become veritable enemies on the football field, battling for city bragging rights.

210

The choice stays with you, echoes forward to the years beyond your high school days. Most likely, your boys will attend the school you chose, and their boys will, too, and so on and so on. Of course, some alumni like to say they don't pay much mind to that rivalry anymore, dismissing it as the stuff of arrested adolescence. But get them alone or gathered with a group of classmates, and you can see the enjoyable antagonism rise, encapsulating a symbolic story of the Old Guard (Ignatius, founded in 1886, Society of Jesus, nine state football titles, and Brian Dowling) against the Young Upstarts (Edward, founded in 1949, Brothers of the Holy Cross, two state-runner-up trophies, and Phil Donahue), or the Wildcats against the Eagles.

Through the years, each team has enjoyed a period of dominance. In the '70s and '80s, the Eagles ran the table behind stifling defenses and hard-nosed running backs like Joe Portale, Frank Waite, and Chris Williams. The '90s ushered in the "Chico" era,

211

reversing the grain, not only for St. Edward, but for all of Division 1 football, as Chuck Kyle's gridiron factory matured and took shape in the form of a pro-style offense, cannon-armed quarterbacks, and players with unsurpassed composure and confidence. And yet, despite the dominance of either team at any point in time, it was quite common to see them end the year with a loss or two, one of those coming at the hands of their most despised rival. Tom Cousineau starred at linebacker for St. Edward in the '70s before going on to an All-American college career at Ohio State and seven years in the NFL and CFL. What's his most coveted memory of playing for St. Edward? "My class never lost to St. Ignatius."

Billy Kahl attended St. Angela Merici grade school in Fairview Park, graduating in a class which he says split 50-50 between St. Edward and St. Ignatius. Like his father and older brother, Kahl went to St. Edward and played quarterback in the early 1980s. During his senior year, the Eagles and Wildcats were tied at halftime of their annual meeting. As the Eagles took the field for the second half, Kahl noticed starting safety Brian Hippler jogging along, crying silently inside his helmet. *What had happened?* Kahl wondered. *Had a coach bawled him out? Had he suffered an injury and been driven to tears by the pain? Had some deep-rooted, off-the-field problem picked the worst time of all to surface?* Kahl asked Hippler what was wrong. "Billy," he answered tearfully, "we just gotta win this game!" And as you think back to Keenan and Kerr sharing a light moment on the gridiron, you appreciate how they laid down their differences, at least for one night.

Rivalries. What are they, exactly? Aren't they just contrived hostilities produced as a way of making our own group seem more special and more right? Aren't they just ways

212

210. Mansfield Ontario v. Castalia Margaretta, W.W. Skiles Field, Shelby, 11/10/01

211. Mogadore v. Maria Stein Marion Local, Paul Brown Tiger Stadium, 12/1/01

212. Cincinnati St. Xavier v. Cleveland St. Ignatius, Canton Fawcett Stadium, 12/1/01

to pump enthusiasm into a sporting event like a manufactured melee at a pre-fight press conference? I mean, we're adults here. We can get past these little differences, can't we?

In the 1800s, the cities of Troy and Piqua were campaigning for the county seat in Miami County down in southwest Ohio. Legend has it that on the night prior to the big decisions, leaders from Troy treated state officials to an evening on the town, plying them with food and much drink and, perhaps not surprisingly, they were given the county seat. Immediately, workers began erecting a stately administration building in the center of Troy to reflect the honor of being chosen for such an important position, made all the more important by the fact that Piqua was the town not chosen. Legend also has it that as the building neared completion, the "Goddess of Justice" was placed on top, scales in hand, her derriere intentionally and symbolically facing north to Piqua. In the days to follow, leaders of Piqua caught wind of the Troy's underhanded tactics and voiced their displeasure across the Miami County plains, a displeasure that still manifests itself annually in the yearly football match-up between the Trojans and Indians.

> " I TOLD MY WIFE THAT
>   AS LONG AS I'M
> COACHING FOOTBALL,
> I'M STAYING IN OHIO."
>
> Chad Ross, Assistant Coach, Crooksville H.S.

There are older rivalries in Ohio. Massillon Washington and Canton McKinley is the oldest and most famous, going strong since 1894. Cincinnati Walnut Hills and Cincinnati Woodward, Dover and New Philadelphia, even Troy and Sidney, have rivalries that go farther back than Troy and Piqua. But for many years, Troy and Piqua played twice a season, and due to this doubling up, they have played more times than any other pair of teams in Ohio, and third most in the nation. Perhaps

213

213. Windham at Southington
     Chalker, 8/25/01

214. Bedford St. Peter Chanel v.
     Marion Pleasant, Canton
     Fawcett Stadium, 11/30/01

215. McComb v. Columbus Grove,
     Lima Stadium, 11/17/01

even more remarkable is that after 117 meetings, the record for this rivalry stands at 56-55 (with six ties) in favor of Troy.

Separated by 10 miles of Interstate 75, the residents of Troy and Piqua have mellowed considerably toward each other through the years. Too many inter-marriages have spoiled the neat divisions between the towns, as have too many people needing employment and traveling to the other town for available work. As the meaning of the rivalry is passed down to the younger generations, the effects have been diluted. Says one young Trojan selling programs for the student council, "You know, it's what we've always grown up with. Not liking Piqua." The Hatfields and McCoys it isn't, but that's not to say it isn't the biggest game of the year for both teams. Any player or resident will tell you that it is, and both towns do their best to give the game a healthy sense of drama. On the Wednesday before the game, the mayors of Troy and Piqua meet at the 50-yard line of the stadium hosting that year's game and trade good-natured barbs before placing a friendly wager on the contest. Ticket lines form the night before the game, tailgates appear, and people camp out beneath the stars in the surrounding parking lots and fields.

At the 2001 pep rally in Troy, Dave Arbogast collected money from students. For a couple bucks, they could take one minute's worth of sledgehammer whacks at a rusty old car painted Piqua blue and red. Some students took full-bodied swings at the car, leaving fresh dents in the steel hull, while others struggled with the unwieldy sledge and desperately tried not to look weak in front of their classmates. The money raised went to the Troy activities fund, and Arbogast was pleased to have been there because his son, a wide receiver and defensive back for the Trojans, was one who would benefit.

214

215

Each student tried to outdo the one before, brandishing a new angle from which to attack the car. Some went for the doors and trunk which seem to crumple more easily. Others stood on the hood and pounded downward, like Thor throwing lightning bolts from the sky. Each swing elicited a chorus of cheers. Arbogast enjoyed the atmosphere, but his mind was a couple miles away at his home. He knew that as he stood there collecting money, friends from Piqua — his wife's hometown — were decorating his home, looping blue and red crepe paper over tree branches, posting Piqua signs on the windows and front door. One year, these spirited marauders did such an impressive job that their handiwork landed Arbogast's home on the front page of the local paper, only inspiring greater house attacks in the years to follow.

Arbogast has tried to mount counter-offensives on several Piqua homes, but his targets have successfully anticipated these moves. His maneuvers have ended in fruitless stand-offs, confrontations with men and women armed with hoses and water balloons. He came away wet and without proper revenge. So as he stood there, imagining what his home would look like this year, he hatched a new plan, the 2001 attack. He went to Piqua after the pep rally and endured his requisite abuse from the Indian fans, and then, after bidding farewell, making them believe that this Troy resident had been roundly defeated, he returned in the night to carry out his master plan — decorating his antagonists' homes in Troy silver and red.

Rivalries. Can we get past our little differences? Yes. But it's not nearly as much fun.

Round three playoff games are filling the portal space now, the regional finals. Columbus Grove and McComb are first up, and in this scene McComb has the ball on offense deep

216

216. Kenton v. Coldwater, Findlay Donnell Stadium, 11/24/01

217. Lincoln-West v. Cleveland East, Patrick Henry Field, 10/12/01

218. Mentor Lake Catholic v. Columbus St. Francis DeSales, Paul Brown Tiger Stadium, 11/30/01

inside Columbus Grove territory. Senior quarterback Dusty Aldrich breaks the huddle, trots up to the line, and surveys the defense with a quick turn of his head. For four years, Dusty has been throwing to his trusty wideout, Rusty Aldrich, who doubles as a twin brother. With McComb's pass-happy offense well-known throughout the Blanchard Valley Conference, every opponent knew the Aldrich brothers would be looking for each other, but still the Panthers moved downfield like a slalom champion in fresh snow. Those who believe in the ability of twins to communicate telepathically should add the 191 Aldrich-to-Aldrich connections to their argument. Observers said there had to be something beyond the tangible at work when Dusty dropped back to pass. For one, neither Aldrich cuts a necessarily intimidating figure. Athletic, yes; intimidating, no. For another, they both approach game time with an extreme relaxation bordering on indifference that gives head coach Kris Alge the unique problem of getting his players *more excited* for the game. Pre-game mood doesn't seem to matter much, however. Three straight trips to the playoffs, and nearly two miles of passing yards later, the Aldrich brothers work together on a level perhaps understood only by sport's special duos — the silent vocabulary of meeting eyes, subtle gestures, and plain old vibe.

217

On this play, however, the Aldrich connection is equally effective as a decoy. With the ball on the Columbus Grove 7-yard line and Rusty split wide to the right, opposite fellow receiver Eric Tracy, Dusty catches the snap from Nathan Westernbarger and drops back to pass. While looking downfield, he bounces slightly on

218

draw for the community as a whole. You won't get 200 Trimble residents driving to Athens for a movie, but you might see double that number in the football stadium on any given Friday night. Irwin says talk has recently surfaced about another merger, possibly with a larger school like Nelsonville-York located seven miles away. The community, she says, will fight this consolidation for the same reasons they resisted the last one: not wanting to lose this local source of entertainment, civic pride, and employment (the largest for both cities), and needing the sense of tradition and stability already compromised once before.

Irwin cares. Like all teachers, she cares. She cares about how well we prepare children for life beyond school. She cares that her school has all the right methods in place to insure that students are imbued with a general sense of right and wrong and a desire to contribute to the larger whole. In history classes, we celebrate people — Eleanor Roosevelt, George Washington Carver, Gandhi — who understood that their talents and ideas were best utilized when engaged with the greater good in mind. Football, any coach will tell you, promotes that ideal. More than anyone on the field tonight, coaches believe in football's capacity to produce healthy, selfless, and industrious citizens for public life. Eleven men dedicated to one goal, sublimating their individual wants for a collective purpose. Teamwork.

In other sports, one player can control a game. In baseball, a dominant pitcher can blow down batters like straw figurines. In basketball, one player can thin out a zone with long-distance shooting or disrupt an offensive scheme with shot-blocking prowess. In hockey or soccer, a hot goalie can make the net appear the size of a mouse hole. This is not to

221

221. Painesville Riverside at
   Columbus St. Francis DeSales,
   9/15/01

222. Cincinnati Archbishop Moeller
   at Cincinnati Elder, 10/5/01

say all these sports don't require some element of teamwork for success, but none of them has its entire success dictated by that fact. Your running back might be 6'3," 220 pounds, and run a 4.2 40-yard dash, but there's no way he's going to beat 11 guys all by himself. Yes, it's probably been done on a single play before, but over the course of the game, any football player will need some help — a teammate to open a hole, assist on a tackle, or run some interference.

At this point in the season, only the real "teams" remain. A few schools scampered into the playoffs on the strength of a few star athletes. But those teams have been summarily dismissed, their conquerors only needing to focus on those particular players to shut down the whole works.

Back on the field, the gridiron portal goes fuzzy for a moment. When it clears, the Firebirds of Bedford St. Peter Chanel have the ball on offense, standing tall and looking fearsome. Across the way, the upstart Seminoles from Woodsfield Monroe Central line up on defense. This scene has been pulled from the state semifinals, week 14 of the high school season. How fitting it is to see the Seminoles setting up to stop the Firebirds' high-powered offensive machine. This is their first trip to the state playoffs, and in the three playoff games leading up to Chanel, Monroe Central shut out two opponents while holding a third to just a field goal.

The Seminoles have not, however, seen an offense the likes of Chanel. The Firebirds, a Division 5 team making its third playoff appearance in a row, averaged over 30 points a game during the regular season, posting impressive wins over several opponents from

higher divisions. At the heart of this attack is Tony Franklin, a 185-pound tailback who will finish the season with well over 2,000 yards rushing and the state championship single-game record of 393 yards. The Firebirds have tasted the state title game before, losing to Amanda-Clearcreek in 2000, but that second-place trophy only fueled their collective desire for state champion hardware.

On the sidelines, Chanel head coach Bill Powers worries about Franklin tonight. Two days prior to this game, Franklin's father died from a stroke suffered the previous week. Franklin contemplated sitting out the Monroe Central game and spending that time with his mother in the stands. But in the end, the young man knew he belonged on the field, exactly where his father would have wanted him to be, on that open green, where from high above the field, Glenn Franklin could watch his son lead the Firebirds to a second straight championship game appearance.

The Seminoles, dressed like their namesake Florida State, are game and determined, but physically outmatched. A couple thousand of their fans made the long trek up to Lowell Klinefelter Stadium in Canton to watch their team take another exploratory step toward Ohio high school football history, but it would not happen tonight. As you watch, the Firebirds drive 53 yards, capping the drive with a one-yard touchdown plunge by Franklin. As he hands the ball off to a waiting official, Franklin points skyward and reflects for a moment while his teammates swirl around him with congratulatory pats and shoves.

At the end of the 2001 season, the Firebirds would earn Chanel's first state football title with a decisive win over a tremendous Marion Pleasant team. Coach Powers would add

223

223. Gnadenhutten Indian Valley at
     Uhrichsville Claymont, 10/27/01

224. Lincoln West v. Cleveland East,
     Patrick Henry, 10/12/01

225. McComb v. Columbus Grove,
     Lima Stadium, 11/17/01

another laurel to this already great achievement by joining Todd Schulte of Delphos St. John's, and a scant few others, in winning a state title in just his first year.

On the sidelines tonight, you've seen several memorable coaches. Earlier in the night you watched Jim France from Akron Manchester walk the sidelines, clad in Panther black and red. With 244 victories in 30-plus years of coaching, he's among the top ten winningest active coaches in Ohio, having led the Panthers to 12 playoff appearances in the last 13 years, and regular title contention in the Principals Athletic Conference.

The winningest coach in Ohio high school football is also its leading active coach, the only head coach Hamilton Stephen T. Badin High School has ever employed. In 44 years, Terry Malone has racked up 353 wins (.760 lifetime percentage) with 15 trips to the state playoffs, one state title, two state runners-up, and even more remarkable, only two losing seasons. It wasn't even called Badin when Malone began his reign. It was Hamilton Catholic, a now-forgotten all-male school that in 1966 merged with Notre Dame Academy, a neighboring young women's high school.

> "FOR EVERY KID THAT GIVES YOU TROUBLE, THERE ARE TEN YOU WANT TO TAKE HOME AND ADOPT. THAT'S THE REASON YOU KEEP DOING THIS. IT'S NOT ABOUT WINS AND LOSSES. IF THEY'RE GOING TO COME OUT, WE'RE GOING TO BE HERE TO COACH THEM."
>
> Jeff Mitchell, Head Coach,
> Akron Central-Hower H.S.

For Malone, the intrigue of a new season, a clean slate with ten open slots, brings him back to the practice field every summer. He loves to practice. Loves it. In fact, Badin's athletic director, Sally Kocher, says Malone only plays the games because he has to. He'd practice all the time if he could. Malone loves the

224

225

grind, the long hours, the attention to detail, and the pursuit of that elusive "best." That oppressive solar energy during two-a-day practices transforms young boys into men, turns brash adolescents into thinking, responsible adults. Many years ago a Badin graduate who had recently returned from Vietnam tracked down his old coach. The young man told Malone it was rigors of summer practices that had given him the mental toughness to endure what he did in the jungles of Southeast Asia.

With all that experience under his hat, Malone doesn't wax eloquent about the appeal of football. As he speaks, you understand that for him, football's positive influence is self-evident, about as meaningful a question as *why do babies make us smile?* If it has to be explained, you probably wouldn't understand. As for football's grip on Ohio, Malone believes it's the industrial roots that have fostered our predilection for gridiron contests. Once a good team formed — the Massillons, McKinleys, Newark Catholics, Moellers, Irontons, Steubenvilles, St. Henry's, and Fostorias — the tradition was built, and the rest just fell into place. That appears to be the case at Badin.

The coaches tonight are constant motion and consultation. They trudge up and down the field exchanging quick words with each other, calling together innumerable ad hoc conferences on the sideline benches, scribbling madly on wipe-it boards, shouting instructions and encouragement to their teams, negotiating and pleading with officials, focusing their incisive eyes on the chaos. Coaches see things differently than we do. Where we see a fullback plow off-tackle for six yards, they see three additional running plays that might exploit that same weakness, or a play-action pass to catch the defense

226

227

offguard. Like chess players, they look for patterns, not plays; they visualize the game in moves ahead of the one taking place.

It's an unwritten rule that in spite of all the dedication coaches demonstrate during the course of a year, they will be showered with blame when things go poorly and expected to deflect all praise when things go right. The whole situation, on its face, appears to be no-win. Pressure builds. Teams lose. Inevitably, they lose. Every team will lose, and yet, in the stands, people snipe loudly within earshot of the coach's family, who feign poor hearing or indifference to public opinion. Every town wants a winner, no one more than the head coach, although sometimes it appears that some people forget that. As Cliff Hite from Findlay once remarked, "No matter how much pressure a town puts on its coach, there's not a coach in the world who doesn't put even more pressure on himself."

Hite would know. He once started his own son at quarterback ahead of a junior, Ben Rothlisberger, who would go on to set several state passing records. People knew Rothlisberger would be a great talent, but Hite went with his son anyway. Never mind that Hite's coaching staff was in complete agreement with his decision to start his son. Never mind that Ryan Hite was named player of the year in his conference and finished his career as the second-leading passer in Findlay High School history. Never mind that Findlay won the Great Lakes League that year under Hite's son's leadership. When Rothlisberger went on to throw 54 touchdown passes the following season (including eight in one game), retroactive criticism flooded through the wrought iron gates of Donnell Stadium, as did accusations of favoritism and nepotism, and ques-

228

226. Crooksville at Chesapeake, 11/2/01

227. Columbus Bishop Watterson v. Lexington, Mt. Vernon Yellow Jacket Stadium, 11/9/01

228. Cincinnati Moeller at Cincinnati Elder, 10/5/01

tions about Hite's ability to coach. Hite, who also teaches American history in Findlay schools, walked around beleaguered, or as he likes to say, "feeling like [he] was on double-secret probation." Like all good coaches, he's developed the requisite thick skin and selective short-term memory. And the town appears to have forgiven him as well. In 2001, he was elected to chair the United Way's annual campaign for Hancock County. Only in Ohio.

The time remaining in the fourth quarter slowly winnows away as the log of games you've seen tonight now reaches into the hundreds. The state finals materialize on the field. At last, the top of the mountain, the party of parties. The Ohio High School Athletic Association's football state finals are a two-day festival stacked with games from eleven in the morning to eleven at night, six games shared between two sites. The most devout fans take personal days from work and caravan back and forth between Massillon's Paul Brown Tiger Stadium and Canton Fawcett Stadium. For many, the state finals pose a lengthy early morning trek from the nether reaches of Ohio to the heart of modern football's birthplace. But once you step out of your vehicle and catch a whiff of that championship air, you know without a doubt your long drive will be rewarded.

Mentor Lake Catholic and Columbus St. Francis DeSales take the field, two Division 3 powerhouses who have 23 post-seasons appearances between them. This year, however, both teams had to overcome serious lumps during the regular season. The Cougars of Lake Catholic earned their spot in the finals with improved play during the playoffs, which required a victory over Cleveland Benedictine, a team

229

229. Kenton v. Coldwater, Findlay Donnell Stadium, 11/24/01

230. Gnadenhutten Indian Valley at Uhrichsville Claymont, 10/27/01

231. Toledo Woodward at Toledo Libbey, 10/27/01

that had shut out the Cougars eight weeks prior. Meanwhile, football observers might have accused St. Francis DeSales of playing dead during their regular season. The Stallions dropped their last four games, giving up an average of nearly 30 points per contest. Yet, thanks to a fearless schedule that featured seven games against teams from higher divisions, DeSales claimed the last available spot in the playoffs with just a 5-5 record before rolling over four straight opponents. Lake Catholic and DeSales played the first game of the 2001 state finals, and it turned out to be its most exciting one as well.

When the portal tunes into this game, the Stallions lead 21-14. Lake Catholic has the ball in DeSales territory with less than five minutes to play. DeSales had jumped out to an early 14-0 lead behind a triple option offense that ran smoother than fine silk. Quarterback Dino Razzano, along with running backs De'Wayne Penn and Tyler Gergley, kept the Cougars on their heels most of the afternoon with sharp fakes and quick-hitting execution. Lake Catholic stepped up in the second quarter with a score, and tied the game at 14 late in the third quarter on a disputed touchdown run by sophomore quarterback Mark Petruziello (DeSales felt Petruziello had gone out of bounds at the 1-yard line). The Stallions responded to that controversy with a masterful drive, going 83 yards in 12 plays to regain the lead with 7:36 to play.

Compared to earlier this evening, the mood change in the stadium is palpable. On both sidelines, the conversations between coaches and players have become more urgent and clipped. There are fewer smiles and less back-slapping going on, less milling about the water cooler, less reminiscing about the previous series of plays.

230

231

Everyone is on his feet and pressed up against the sidelines. The officials remind the coaches (for the 17th time) to keep their players three yards off the sidelines. Shorter players stand on tip-toe and crane their necks to see the action. In the stands, the running dialogues that once streamed freely through the rows have ended. Stiff-jawed and thin-lipped, the spectators have taken a renewed interest in the action.

Petruziello breaks the huddle for Lake Catholic. The Cougars are facing a fourth down and 10 at the DeSales 40-yard line. Across the line, sophomore linebacker Austin Addington, who appeared to make nearly every tackle in the first half, stands poised on his toes, ready for pursuit. Split ends Matt Matteucci and Mark Watson flank opposite sides of the Cougar offense. As the running game has carried the Stallions, so has the passing game lifted Lake Catholic. Between Matteucci and Watson, they already have 14 catches on the day for over 200 yards, and there's still time remaining.

For the moment, the dark mood of the Lake Catholic fans has lifted and the chatter returns. Now the DeSales faithful are bracing, hoping for a break, a big play, plain dumb luck, anything to stop this drive. Petruziello takes the snap and drops back. Fullback Dan Cvelbar sets up to block in front of his quarterback. Matteucci and Watson break downfield and look for open spots in DeSales' zone coverage defense. The play takes time to develop. The Cougars need 10 yards. Not eight, not nine-and-a-half, but ten. As Petruziello waits for a receiver to break open, the white-jerseyed Stallion defenders close around him like a noose. Ordinarily, he'd think about throwing the ball away, but this time, he'll have to keep it, or toss it desperately up for grabs.

232

233

Watson runs at the safety, trying to draw him away from the middle where Matteucci should arrive a second later.

Petruziello anticipates the right moment. Just as Stallion defenders have the quarterback at arm's length, he throws the ball straight down the middle of the field. It's a high throw, and the spiral wobbles a bit, but it's right on target. Matteucci leaps into the air and pulls it down for a 13-yard gain and a first down. A few plays later, Petruziello and Matteucci hook up again, this time for a touchdown, sending the game into overtime. The Cougars have found extra life.

While neither team has the game won at this point, it's the Cougars who have a noticeably lighter step when overtime begins. Through some luck and sheer guts, they have found themselves with a chance to win after things looked so bleak in the fourth quarter. The Stallions, however, do not hang their heads. Just five weeks ago, they were praying to the playoff gods for another chance, and they got it. With three state title banners hanging in their gym on Karl Road in north Columbus, they're confident they can bring home a fourth.

DeSales takes the ball first on offense. They start from the Lake Catholic 20-yard line. As the Stallions come to the line, the fans rise to their feet with a collective roar that sounds strangely like static from your television set. DeSales calls a pass play. Razzano looks for his brother, senior Patsy, on a fade route up the left sideline. Matteucci, who plays both ways, defends the play perfectly. The elder Razzano never has a chance. Matteucci picks the ball out of the air and tumbles down into the end zone, snuffing

234

232. Piqua at Troy, 9/21/01

233. Mansfield Ontario v. Castalia Margaretta, W.W. Skiles Field, Shelby, 11/10/01

234. Lakewood St. Edward v. Cleveland St. Ignatius, Lakewood Stadium, 10/13/01

out the Stallions' hopes, at least for now. The crowd's deafening roar turns into a wail.
Lake Catholic fans trade hugs and blow out their cheeks in mock relief. DeSales fans
wring their hands and look skyward in exasperation — so close it was.

The Cougars keep this momentum for their series on offense. On first down, Petruziello
and Matteucci connect for 13 yards and a first down. With the ball on the DeSales
seven-yard line, third-year head coach Tom Lombardo decides to keep the ball on the
ground for the next two plays, allowing his fullback Cvelbar to lunge forward for four
difficult but momentous yards. As Woody Hayes once said, "Three things can happen
when you pass, and two of them ain't good." Apparently Lombardo, with a state title
now just three yards away, feels this is sound advice.

It's third and goal for Lake Catholic when Petruziello calls the next play. The Stallions
await the Cougars at the line. Light steam purls out the front of their helmets as they
hop up and down to stay loose, waiting for the snap. Their teammates yell final encouragement. They slap shoulder pads and turn to each other with wide open expressions,
feeling the joy of this moment: state championship game, overtime, tied at 21. How
many times they created this scenario while playing in the backyard, imagining a stadium filled with screaming fans, surrounded by their friends, teammates, poised to
become heroes, ready to accept the result, victory or defeat, ecstasy or dejection.

On the sidelines, players hold hands; others take a knee. They stand close together
and feel in this moment, more than any other tonight, what it's like to be part of a
team. Hours upon hours upon hours of strain and sweat come to these few plays. It's not

235

235. Alexander Stadium, Piqua, 9/21/01

236. Crooksville at Chesapeake, 11/2/01

fair, but you knew that coming in. They're prepared for any outcome. Whether the Cougars score on this possession, or if DeSales gets the ball back and converts a score, half the players in this stadium will share in victory. The victors will congratulate and praise one another, brimming with raw enthusiasm and love. The other half will summon up reserves of quiet strength, trying to cope with the harsh reprisal of defeat. And for a fleeting instant, you'll see the pinnacle of football's effect on youth, the part that allows them to act not like the steely, disaffected young men they learn to be on television, but rather like the sensitive, communicative, passionate human beings we all wish we could be more often.

In the stands, you look at the woman standing next to you. She teeters back and forth, rocking trance-like, staring at her feet. She can't bear to watch. Two men in front of you affect stoic faces while their knees flex up and down, up and down. The band and cheerleaders have clumped together, linking arms, their muscles tense, their hearts racing. Young girls let out convulsive shrieks. Your heart sings. You want to shout out above this crowd, to convey your appreciation for this moment, this splendidly taut moment that you'll savor and savor until next year. *Thank you! Thank you for having me! I'm having a great time!*

The center fires the ball back through his legs. The lines collide a final time, forcefully, desperately. The offensive linemen go low, trying to open a seam somewhere in this writhing mass of players. The defense bursts forward with all their might, looking for the ball while holding off blockers. Petruziello catches the snap and hands off to Cvelbar, placing the ball squarely between the "2" and "0" of his uniform. The fullback

disappears in a morass of plastic-coated bodies. Helmets and shoulder pads crack against one another like electrical slaps. The woman next to you gasps. Cvelbar churns his legs and surges forward. DeSales pushes back, creating a momentary stalemate in this reverse tug-of-war. Cvelbar gets hit from the side, but still he's upright. Stallion arms and hands clutch at him frantically, grasping for a shirt tail, a shoe top, or belt loop — anything to deter his progress. The Cougar line drives forward and slips, drives forward and slips, drives forward and slips, inch by inch they go. Cvelbar falls, his legs still churning for yards. He crashes to the ground unaware of his status, having lost track in the howling panic that was the center of the line. A whistle blast!
And glorious celebration ensues.

This game, you think to yourself, *it's a wonderful thing. A truly wonderful thing.*

237

238

TUF-WEAR®
DIAL-A-DOWN™

237. Struthers at Niles McKinley, 10/11/01

238. Cincinnati St. Xavier v. Cleveland St. Ignatius,
     Canton Fawcett Stadium, 12/1/01

239. Ashland Mapleton at Plymouth, 10/26/01

ACROSS MANY FIELDS

240. Bedford St. Peter Chanel v. Marion Pleasant, Canton Fawcett Stadium, 11/30/01

241. Toledo St. Francis DeSales v. Columbus Bishop Watterson, Paul Brown Tiger Stadium, 11/30/01

242. Bedford St. Peter Chanel v. Marion Pleasant, Canton Fawcett Stadium, 11/30/01

243. Bedford St. Peter Chanel v. Marion Pleasant, Canton Fawcett Stadium, 11/30/01

POSTGAME

242

IT WASN'T LONG AGO that you were anxious and lost, muttering angrily at your limited Internet map. The town looked strange and deserted. The stadium was elusive and the humidity oppressive. You mocked yourself for driving all this way to a high school football game.

How times have changed! Now you're chatting it up with the woman next to you, cracking jokes, telling personal stories. She listens intently and laughs heartily at everything you say, touching your arm with neighborly affection. Her eyes beam with exhilaration, still reeling from the spectacle on the field. She wears a powder blue toque and powder blue mittens and carries a matching seat cushion. Her voice, weakened by two hours of shouting and cheering, strains to be heard above the postgame walla walla. *When you come this far, how can one team lose? I mean, how can you feel like there are any losers tonight? I just can't believe it! What a game! I'm spent.* You agree. And

243

here you are, standing in the cold that you once felt with escalating resentment. It comforts you now like a stage prop perfectly selected for this final scene of the night.

On the field, six teams — six groups of champions — circulate amidst a welter of fans. The players walk around starry-eyed, seeking out hugs, and searching for words. Their faces are battle-streaked, eye black mixed with sweat, like actors who removed only half their makeup. Their bodies are relaxed once more, and they look like kids again. Coaches guffaw loudly, shake hands, and pose for pictures. Parents, cloaked in school

244. Mentor Lake Catholic v. Columbus St. Francis DeSales, Paul Brown Tiger Stadium, 11/30/01

245. New Middletown Springfield at Poland Seminary, 8/24/01

244

colors, search out familiar faces. Some cry while others show thin smiles and trill with ineffable pride. The cheerleaders, band, and classmates romp like frolicking puppies, laughing and screaming, their contagious joy filling up and spilling over the sides of this amazing stadium.

Just minutes ago, officials from the OHSAA handed out 12 awards — six second-place trophies and six championship models. Speaking into field mikes, they offered fulsome praise and reassurance to the runners-up, and hearty congratulations to the winners. Their words echoed loudly, interspersed with applause from both sides of the stadium. Teams huddled around barely listening, not out of disregard, but more from distraction due to the immensity of the moment.

When the Ohio high school playoffs began in 1972, only three teams could win championships in either Class A, Class AA, or Class AAA. Over the years, the OHSAA expanded the number of divisions to five and then six in an effort to create parity between schools with different enrollment numbers. In 2001, there were six divisions. Six titles to be won. Six team champions crowned. The names change from year to year. This year they would be known as Wildcats (Cleveland St. Ignatius), Knights (Toledo St. Francis DeSales), Cougars (Mentor Lake Catholic), Wildcats (Kenton), Firebirds (Bedford St. Peter Chanel), and Flyers (Maria Stein Marion Local).

Chuck Kyle and his St. Ignatius Wildcats moved their dynasty a step further, claiming their ninth state Division 1 title, (the most by any school in the state), but perhaps none

was sweeter than this year's. St. Ignatius scrambled through the regular season, losing three of its last four games (two of those in overtime). Injuries plagued the team early in the year, but when the playoffs arrived, like all great teams, the Wildcats found their stride again.

Early in 2001, head coach Dick Cromwell told Rodney Gamby he would play tailback for Toledo St. Francis DeSales. Gamby had wanted to play tight end, but Cromwell's decision prevailed, and no one will doubt the coach again. Gamby gained 2,000 yards on his way to picking up all-state accolades. Combined with a mighty defense, the Knights stormed through the playoffs to the Division 2 crown, 17 years after winning their first state title.

Ten years ago, John Gibbons coached Lake Catholic to its first state title. This year he stood on the sidelines, watching his son-in-law Tom Lombardo lead the Cougars to the school's third state championship trophy. The family affair ran onto the field as well. In the middle of the Lake Catholic defense, linebacker Mike Gibbons (son of John, brother-in-law of Tom), listed at a less-than-frightening 165 pounds, played 40 pounds heavier and won Division 3 defensive player-of-the-year honors.

Kenton fans and head coach Mike Mauk waited. In 18 years, Mauk led the Wildcats to just two playoff appearances in Division 4. Other coaches may have fretted during this long dry spell, but Mauk had an ace in his pocket; he just needed some time. The ace arrived in 2001. His son, Benjamin, wowed the entire Buckeye state, throwing to an awesomely talented group of receivers and breaking the national record for single-season passing yardage with 5,542. And the Wildcat band plays: *1-2-3-4, who are you rooting for? Kenton, that's who!*

246

In 2000, it had been so close for Bedford St. Peter Chanel. Led by then-head coach Jeff Rotsky, they defeated two powerful teams (New Middletown Springfield and Liberty Center) on the way to the state final before losing to head coach Ron Hinton and the Amanda-Clearcreek Aces. They preserved and nurtured that disappointment for one year before unleashing it on every opponent they encountered in 2001. Hard-hitting linebackers T. Terry and Kyle Hoogenboom insured that Chanel's opponents understood their place in the Division 5 world of Ohio high school football — behind the Firebirds.

247

In Division 6, rumors of another west central Ohio dynasty have emerged. In five post-season games, Marion Local (Or is it Maria Stein?) outscored their opponents 203-20 en route to a second straight state championship. Junior quarterback Chad Otte and senior linebacker Nathan Kuether marshaled a balanced attack for the Flyers on both sides of the ball. Head coach Tim Goodwin, in just his third year, brought Marion Local from relative anonymity to statewide recognition. Located in Maria Stein, no one mistakes the name of the school for the name of the town anymore.

Off to the side of the field, toward the end zone, a second group of teams huddles in small packs. There is less noise here and far fewer smiles. The hugs in this area have a different shape: they're long and droopy, compared to the ones at midfield which are zealous and full-bodied. These teams, too, have names that change from year to year. In 2001, they're known as Bombers (Cincinnati St. Xavier), Eagles (Columbus Bishop Watterson), Stallions (Columbus St. Francis DeSales), Panthers (Newark Licking

248

246. Columbus World Harvest Academy v. Yellow Springs, Pickerington Stadium, 9/15/01

247. Mentor Lake Catholic v. Columbus St. Francis DeSales, Paul Brown Tiger Stadium, 11/30/01

248. Cincinnati St. Xavier v. Cleveland St. Ignatius, Canton Fawcett Stadium, 12/1/01

Valley), Spartans (Marion Pleasant), and Wildcats (Mogadore). This year they have known great success, defeated strong opponents, and excelled at being a team. Counted with this season's state champions, they represent less than two percent of all the high school teams in Ohio. Six hundred ninety-six teams were sitting at home during the state finals, waiting to read about these games in the morning paper. Six hundred ninety-six teams fought to be right where these teams are standing now — win or lose. Those same six hundred ninety-six teams will vie for these spots again next year, using these 12 finalists' success as a measuring stick for their own.

No matter how convincing you find these points to be, they provide little or no consolation to tonight's runners-up. Some players weep, and others run through personal grieving processes of denial, anger, and regret. Acceptance comes later: maybe tonight before they turn off the bedroom lights, maybe tomorrow as they talk about the game with their parents over breakfast, or maybe on Monday when they return to school and lose themselves in the once-again-ordinary life of high school students. You know that in no time at all, with the bemusing resiliency of youth, these players will turn this single loss into overall achievement.

The Marion Pleasant Spartans break away from the pack, and form calisthenic rows on the field. Captains Justin Kume and Justin Williams call out the drill. It's a Pleasant tradition to finish each game, win or lose, with a set of jumping jacks. Tonight, they mean more than ever. The state finals would be Pleasant's only loss of the 2001 season. After victories, the Spartans use jumping jacks to show that they would not rest on

"IF YOU'RE GOING TO BASE YOUR SUCCESS ON SOME PIMPLY-FACED 17-YEAR-OLD WHO'S FIGHTING EVERY WEEK WITH HIS GIRLFRIEND, YOU'RE GOING TO HAVE PROBLEMS."

Jim Keating, Staff Photographer, *Cincinnati Enquirer* newspaper

249

249. Kenton v. Newark Licking Valley, Canton Fawcett Stadium, 12/1/01

250. Cincinnati St. Xavier v. Cleveland St. Ignatius, Canton Fawcett Stadium, 12/1/01

251. Piqua at Troy, 9/21/01

their laurels, that they were ready to work toward their next opponent. Tonight, they use the exercise to say that even defeat on the highest stage cannot quash their competitive spirit.

"WE WERE BROUGHT UP TO BELIEVE THAT FOOTBALL IS VERY IMPORTANT. IT WAS A WAY FOR AN INDIVIDUAL TO LEARN ABOUT HIMSELF AND HIS COMMUNITY. IT'S A WAY FOR THE COMMUNITY TO BECOME INVOLVED IN THE KIDS' LIVES. AND I THINK THAT'S THE EMPHASIS WE HAVE HERE IN OHIO... [FOOTBALL IS] PART OF OUR ROOTS AND PART OF OUR ORIGINS. AND SOMETIMES WE MAY NOT UNDERSTAND WHY, BUT WE'RE GLAD IT'S THERE."

Brian Gastin, Head Coach, Mount Vernon H.S.

If you can dream — and not make dreams your master; If you can think — and not make thoughts your aim; If you can meet with triumph and disaster and treat those two imposters just the same. You hear these lines and turn around to identify the speaker. Those words are from a Rudyard Kipling poem you read in high school and haven't heard since. A man stands two rows behind you, focused on the field. When you turn to look at him, he acknowledges you with an easy smile and a short greeting. His voice doesn't match the one you heard reciting the poem. Strange.

The man steps down and joins you for some postgame discussion. His name is Tom Rataiczak and he's from Bellaire. He used to coach basketball, but his role as executive secretary for the Ohio Valley Athletic Conference brings him out to all kinds of high school sporting events. You exchange some brief remarks about the games. Like most Ohio Valley folk, Rataiczak feels at home in a football stadium, and tonight is no exception. The whole evening has been rosy for sure. As the conversation progresses, his tone changes. Rataiczak admits that he has reservations about football's direction from time to time. He sees little things that cause him to pause and wonder if we haven't lost proper perspective on the game.

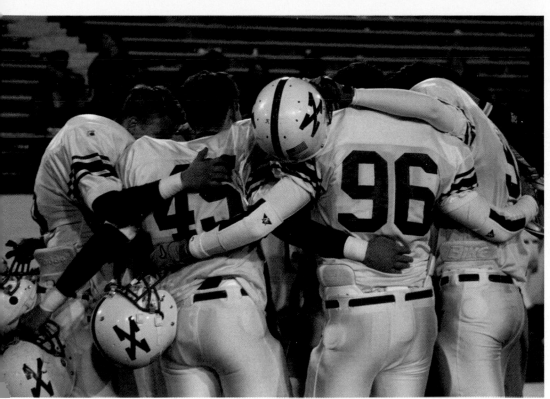

Take summer 2001 in Bellaire, for instance. Rataiczak says the town was building new stands for the football stadium at the same time it was constructing a new middle and elementary school. Both projects were to be completed before the start of the school year. As the summer progressed, it appeared that construction at the sites might not meet the projected deadlines. Then one night, some vandals broke into the new school, destroying tens of thousands of dollars in construction, setting that project back even farther. In the days that followed the incident, Rataiczak says more people appeared concerned that the new football stands might not be completed in time for opening day.

Then there are the parents — as difficult as that is to admit. If there's been one common criticism about high school football, it's the parents. In occasional cases of concern or love gone overboard, they've become too involved, too pushy, and too demanding. Many people see it as a problem of social decay. Cornelius Parson, head coach at Akron East, said to you, "When I played, my dad didn't yell out on the field, 'Hey, hey, my boy should get the ball!' He never did that. He believed in what the coaches were doing. The coaches were with us every day on the field. They knew what we could do." Nearly everyone reaffirms this complaint: players, coaches, officials, athletic directors, administrators, teachers, and even other parents. So what to do? Again, it appears to be a perspective problem. What was that Kipling line? *If you can meet with triumph and disaster and treat those two imposters just the same.*

Rataiczak says goodbye and heads for the exit row. Other spectators follow. They move around you like water around a rock in the river, flowing toward the parking lot and the inevitable return to actual life. Their words are tinged with weary jubilation, multiple lines of game description layering on top of each other, creating a thick weave of memory, a mental fabric that will be carried away from this game and brought out for display at

252

countless events in the future. You want to call after these people, *Until next year, friends! Until next year, when we meet again!*

What about you? Have you fulfilled your mission? Have you discovered why people support high school football in Ohio like no other sport?

Yes, structure.

Every Friday and Saturday night in the fall, you can find a high school football game. It becomes part of your weekend ritual, comforting in its reliability.

Fellowship?

Yes, that's another good reason. We can mingle in the stands, share stories, cheer for our team, and feel like a community.

Escape?

Definitely. Our teams put on weekly shows of athletic drama, performing for us, combining their sacrifice and hard work with our desire to witness the exceptional.

Tradition?

That's probably the strongest reason of all. Our children play the way we played and the way our parents played. The game still requires dedication, determination, and

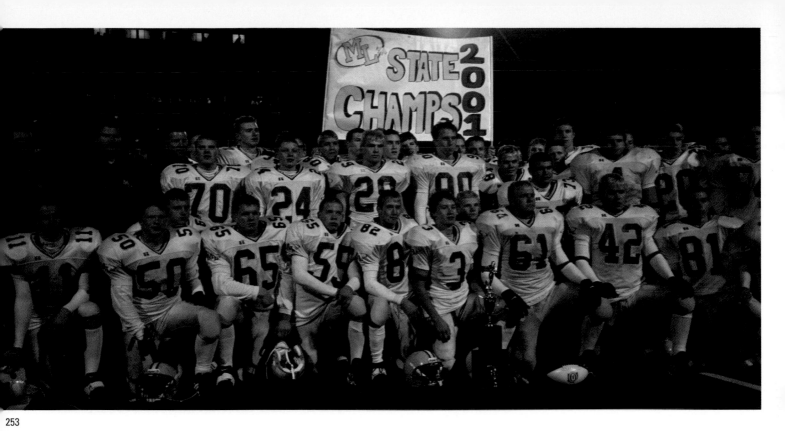

253

perseverance. And when we see these values in action on the field, we take heart knowing they have been sustained at least for one more generation.

The motivations are all so neat and tidy Or are they? Isn't there something more at work here? You've talked to many people, most of whom have been around Ohio high school football longer than you, and even they have trouble giving adequate explanations. Thom McDaniels, head coach at Warren Harding High School, has coached for over 20 years in Ohio, winning a state title and guiding teams that have produced no fewer than 30 Division 1 college players, including his two sons, Josh and Ben. Even he is at a loss for words: "I don't know if I can explain [our state's devotion to high school football], and I should be able to because I'm an English teacher and I should be articulate, but I don't know if I can articulate that. I think that you have to see this. I was part of the Massillon-McKinley rivalry for 18 years, for goodness sakes, and if you've never been to one of those games, you need to go. I can't explain that to you. You have to experience that. I've been involved in big games against Moeller and St. Ignatius, and the electricity in those stadiums is real. The communities get caught up in that. It's real. It's tangible. But I don't know that I can explain it to anyone's satisfaction. You've got to come and see this to believe it."

You're standing alone now. The orange pylons have been pulled off the field, and the gridiron portal has faded to black. The press box has been cleared out, and all the stadium lights have been dimmed. *Nothing to see here, folks.* Just a couple policemen remain on the outskirts of the field, nodding briskly to the final few people who saunter to their cars in the darkened parking lot. As you search for your keys, you think about the long trip ahead of you. Under the black, starry veil of night, you'll

254. New Middletown Springfield at
     Poland Seminary, 8/24/01

255. Cincinnati Colerain, 10/5/01

254

push your car back down the roads that brought you here, scanning the radio dial for talk radio or good cruising music, debating whether or not you should grab a cup of coffee at the gas station, calculating what time you'll arrive at home, wondering who else is on the road at this time of night, but mostly remembering ... remembering the touchdowns and tackles, the handshakes and stories, the high-fives and tears, the music and cheers, all of it resting safely in your heart, all of it bringing a contented smile to your face that will remain there until next season when teams take the field again. We'll see you there.

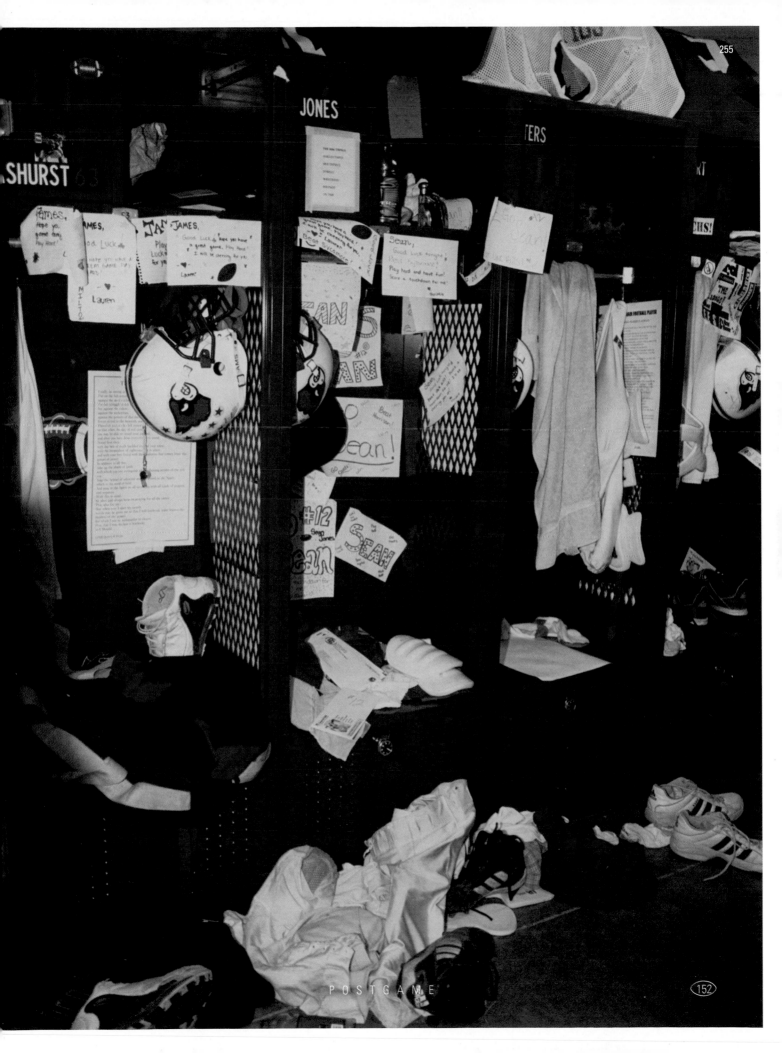

8/23	**Columbiana Crestview** at Lowellville	17-6
8/24	New Middletown Springfield at **Poland Seminary**	19-0
8/25	**Windham** at Southington Chalker	48-12
8/25	Ashtabula Edgewood at **Hanoverton United**	29-12
8/31	Van Wert at **Defiance**	7-6
9/1	**Oregon Cardinal Stritch** at Fostoria St. Wendelin	24-6
9/7	**Waverly** at Wellston	34-30
9/8	Akron Manchester at **Hamilton Badin**	17-12
9/14	**Circleville** at Ashville Teays Valley	26-3
9/15	Yellow Springs at **Columbus World Harvest Christian Academy**	34-13
9/15	Painesville Riverside at **Columbus St. Francis DeSales**	26-7
9/21	**Piqua** at Troy	28-0
9/22	Ada at **Delphos Jefferson**	34-7
9/28	**Granville** at Baltimore Liberty Union	42-41
9/29	**Richmond Edison** at Bellaire	36-6
9/29	**Malvern** at New Philadelphia Tuscarawas Central Catholic	43-14
10/5	Cincinnati Moeller at **Cincinnati Elder**	43-6
10/6	**Portsmouth** at Dayton Meadowdale	47-6
10/11	Struthers at **Niles McKinley**	14-7
10/12	**Cleveland East** at Cleveland Lincoln West	37-6
10/12	**Avon Lake** at Amherst Steele	14-3
10/13	Lorain Southview at **Shaker Heights**	55-14
10/13	Cleveland St. Ignatius at **Lakewood St. Edward**	44-41 (ot)
10/19	East Liverpool at **Steubenville**	21-7
10/20	Akron East at **Akron Central Hower**	12-6
10/20	**Newcomerstown** at Bowerston Conotton Valley	50-0
10/20	**Sandusky Perkins** at Sandusky St. Mary's Central Catholic	27-7
10/26	Ashland Mapleton at **Plymouth**	41-0
10/27	**Toledo Woodward** at Toledo Libbey	6-0
10/27	**Gnadenhutten Indian Valley** at Uhrichsville Claymont	28-21

PLAYOFFS

11/2	**Crooksville** at Chesapeake	35-21
11/3	Reedsville Eastern at **Glouster Trimble**	23-6
11/9	**Columbus Bishop Watterson** v. Lexington (@ Mt. Vernon Yellow Jacket Stadium)	35-7
11/10	**Cincinnati St. Xavier** v. Cincinnati Princeton (@ Paul Brown Stadium)	6-0
11/10	Mansfield Ontario v. **Castalia Margaretta** (@ Shelby W.W. Skiles Field)	13-6
11/16	**Marion Pleasant** v. Liberty Center (@ Findlay Donnell Stadium)	24-0
11/17	McComb v. **Columbus Grove** (@ Lima Stadium)	21-14
11/23	**Bedford St. Peter Chanel** v. Woodsfield Monroe Central (@ Canton Lowell Klinefelter Stadium)	35-0
11/24	**Kenton** v. Coldwater (@ Findlay Donnell Stadium)	49-38

STATE FINALS

11/30	**Mentor Lake Catholic** v. Columbus St. Francis DeSales (@ Massillon Paul Brown Tiger Stadium)	27-21 (ot)
11/30	**Bedford St. Peter Chanel** v. Marion Pleasant (@ Canton Fawcett Stadium)	44-27
11/30	**Toledo St. Francis DeSales** v. Columbus Bishop Watterson (@ Massillon Paul Brown Tiger Stadium)	28-14
12/1	**Kenton** v. Newark Licking Valley (@ Canton Fawcett Stadium)	40-13
12/1	Mogadore v. **Maria Stein Marion Local** (@ Massillon Paul Brown Tiger Stadium)	63-7
12/1	Cincinnati St. Xavier v. **Cleveland St. Ignatius** (@ Canton Fawcett Stadium)	37-6